Broken Promises

Western Hegemony and Global Turmoil

JIBRIL MOHAMED AHMED

Copyright © 2024 Jibril Mohamed Ahmed

All rights reserved.

ISBN:

DEDICATION

To all those who have been marginalized and overlooked in the pursuit of power and progress. To the voices that have been silenced and the communities that have suffered in the name of progress. This book is dedicated to the hope of a more just and equitable world, where promises are kept, and every individual has the opportunity to thrive.

CONTENTS

	Acknowledgments	i.
	Introduction	3
1	Chapter 1: The Historical Foundations of Western Hegemony	3
2	Chapter 2: Imperialism and the Scramble for Africa.	Pg #
3	Chapter 3: The Cold War and Western Interventions	Pg #
4	Chapter 4: The Rise of Globalization and Its Discontents	Pg #
5	Chapter 5: The Impact of Western Hegemony on Global Trade and Economic Policies	Pg #
6	Chapter 6: The Bretton Woods System and Economic Imperialism	Pg #
7	Chapter 7: Cultural Hegemony and the Spread of Western Values	Pg #
8	Chapter 8: The Neoliberal and the Global South	Pg #
9	Chapter 9: The Environmental Consequences of Western Development	Pg #
10	Chapter 10: The Rise of New Powers and the Challenge to Western Hegemony*	Pg #
11	Chapter 11: Broken Promises and the Future of Global Governance	
12	Conclusion: Toward a New Global Order: Lessons from History and the Path Forward	

ACKNOWLEDGMENTS

I begin by expressing my deepest gratitude to Allah, whose guidance and blessings have been my constant source of strength and inspiration throughout this journey. His wisdom has illuminated my path and provided me with the clarity and perseverance needed to complete this work.

I am profoundly grateful to my parents, whose unwavering support, love, and sacrifices have shaped my life and academic endeavors. To my mother and father, your encouragement and belief in me have been a pillar of strength, and I dedicate this achievement to your enduring love and faith.

A heartfelt thank you to my spiritual leader, Sh. Mohamednur Sh. Abdilkadir. Your insightful guidance and spiritual wisdom have been instrumental in shaping my understanding and perspective on the subjects discussed in this book. Your teachings have been a beacon of light in my scholarly and personal life.

To the love of my life, Hanan, your patience, love, and encouragement have been my greatest support throughout this process. Your belief in me has been a constant motivation, and I am forever grateful for your presence and support in my life.

I also extend my sincere thanks to my friends and extended family for their invaluable support and encouragement. Your faith in me, your understanding, and your constant cheerleading have played a crucial role in this journey. Each of you has contributed in your own special way, and for that, I am deeply thankful.

To all of you, I offer my heartfelt appreciation and gratitude.

—*Jibril Mohamed Ahmed*

INTRODUCTION

Broken Promises: Western Hegemony and Global Turmoil

The story of Western hegemony is one of grand promises and profound disillusionment, a tale that has shaped the contours of our modern world in ways both visible and obscure. From the towering spires of European colonial empires to the sprawling reach of American influence, the West has, for centuries, positioned itself as the arbiter of progress, the champion of democracy, and the beacon of human rights. Yet, beneath these lofty ideals lies a complex reality—one marked by exploitation, inequality, and a legacy of turmoil that continues to reverberate across the globe.

The narrative begins in the age of exploration, when European powers first set sail across uncharted waters, driven by a thirst for new lands and resources. The initial encounters with the indigenous peoples of Africa, Asia, and the Americas were marked by a mixture of curiosity and condescension. These "new worlds" were seen as both a threat and an opportunity, inhabited by people who were deemed either noble savages in need of civilization or primitive barbarians to be subdued. The promises made to these peoples, of mutual respect and beneficial trade, were quickly overshadowed by the harsh realities of conquest, slavery, and colonization.

Take, for instance, the story of the Congo under Belgian rule. King Leopold II of Belgium, under the guise of humanitarianism, promised to bring civilization and development to the Congolese people. What followed, however, was one of the most brutal regimes in colonial history. Millions of Congolese were enslaved, tortured, and killed, all in the pursuit of rubber and other resources to fuel the European economy. The promised benefits of Western civilization were revealed to be nothing more than a thin veneer, hiding the ruthless exploitation and violence that underpinned the colonial enterprise.

As the centuries progressed, the promises of the West evolved, but the underlying dynamics remained largely unchanged. The dawn of the 20th century saw the rise of new global powers, with the United States emerging as a key player on the world stage. The rhetoric of freedom and democracy became central to the American identity, particularly during the Cold War, when the U.S. positioned itself as the leader of the "free world" in opposition to the communist bloc. Yet, this period also saw numerous instances where American actions belied its professed values.

In Latin America, for example, the U.S. frequently intervened in the internal affairs of sovereign nations, justifying these actions as necessary to contain the spread of communism. The promise of supporting democratic governance often gave way to the reality of backing authoritarian regimes that were more amenable to American interests. The case of Chile is particularly illustrative. In 1973, the U.S. supported a military coup that overthrew the democratically elected government of Salvador Allende, replacing it with the dictatorship of General Augusto Pinochet. The ensuing years were marked by severe repression, human rights abuses, and economic hardship for the Chilean people—hardly the fruits of the democracy and freedom that the U.S. had promised to uphold.

The post-Cold War era did little to alter the trajectory of Western hegemony. The collapse of the Soviet Union was heralded by many as the "end of history," a moment when liberal democracy and capitalism had triumphed as the ultimate forms of human governance. Yet, the spread of these systems, often imposed through economic pressure or military intervention, has frequently led to destabilization and conflict rather than the peace and prosperity that were promised.

In Iraq, the 2003 U.S.-led invasion was justified on the grounds of liberating the Iraqi people from the tyranny of Saddam Hussein and bringing democracy to the Middle East. What followed was a prolonged period of violence, sectarian conflict, and the rise of extremist groups like ISIS, leaving Iraq in a state of disarray from which it has yet to fully recover. The promise of democracy brought with it a Pandora's box of unintended consequences, exacerbating rather than resolving the underlying tensions within Iraqi society.

Beyond the direct interventions, Western economic policies have also had a profound impact on global stability. The neoliberal model of development, championed by institutions like the International Monetary Fund (IMF) and the World Bank, has been promoted as the key to unlocking economic growth and reducing poverty in the developing world. However, the implementation of these policies often requires austerity measures that disproportionately affect the poor, leading to social unrest and further entrenching inequality.

Greece, a nation that found itself at the mercy of international creditors during the Eurozone crisis, is a stark example of this. The harsh austerity measures imposed by the IMF and the European Union led to widespread unemployment, poverty, and a dramatic decline in living standards. The promise of economic stability and growth through neoliberal reforms turned into a nightmare for many ordinary Greeks, highlighting the disconnect between the theoretical benefits of these policies and their real-world consequences.

The environmental impact of Western hegemony is another area where the promises of progress and development have come into stark conflict with reality. The industrial revolution, which began in the West and has since spread globally, brought with it unprecedented levels of economic growth and technological advancement. However, this progress has come at a tremendous cost to the environment, contributing to climate change, deforestation, and the depletion of natural resources.

The story of the Niger Delta in Nigeria is a case in point. For decades, Western oil companies have extracted vast amounts of oil from this region, promising development and prosperity for the local population. Instead, the Delta has become one of the most polluted regions in the world, with oil spills devastating the local environment and the livelihoods of the people who depend on it. The promised benefits of development have been eclipsed by the environmental destruction and social unrest that have come in its wake.

The cultural impact of Western hegemony is perhaps more subtle but no less significant. The spread of Western media, entertainment, and consumer culture has led to a form of cultural homogenization, where local traditions and identities are increasingly eroded in favor of a globalized, Western-dominated culture. This phenomenon can be seen in the rapid proliferation of Western brands, movies, and music across the world, often at the expense of indigenous cultures and practices.

In India, for example, the influence of Western culture is evident in the changing lifestyles and values of the urban middle class. Traditional practices and beliefs are increasingly being replaced by Western norms, leading to a sense of cultural dislocation and identity crisis among many Indians. The promise of global integration through the adoption of Western culture has, in many cases, led to the loss of cultural diversity and the erosion of local identities.

As we navigate the complexities of the 21st century, it is clear that the promises made by the West—whether in the form of democracy, economic development, or cultural progress—have often fallen short of their mark. The legacy of Western hegemony is one of both achievement and failure, progress and exploitation, enlightenment and oppression. It is a legacy that continues to shape our world in profound ways, as nations and peoples grapple with the consequences of a global order that has been heavily influenced, if not outright dictated, by the West.

This book aims to unpack these contradictions, exploring the ways in which Western hegemony has contributed to global turmoil, even as it has promised a better world. Through a critical examination of history, economics, politics, and culture, we will delve into the complex and often troubling relationship between the West and the rest of the world. By understanding the roots of these broken promises, we can begin to chart a course towards a more equitable and just global future—one that moves beyond the shadow of Western hegemony towards a more inclusive and sustainable world order..

Chapter 1: The Historical Foundations of Western Hegemony

The story of Western hegemony begins not with the global dominance we see today, but with a series of calculated moves that laid the groundwork for an enduring influence over the world. The roots of Western power stretch back to the Age of Exploration, when European nations, driven by a hunger for wealth and resources, began to expand their reach beyond the confines of their own continent. This era marked the beginning of a new world order, one that would be shaped by the relentless pursuit of power, control, and dominance.

During the 15th and 16th centuries, European explorers set sail across the Atlantic, Pacific, and Indian Oceans, driven by the desire to discover new lands and establish trade routes. The so-called "Age of Discovery" was, in reality, an age of conquest. With the backing of powerful monarchs and the financial resources of wealthy merchants, European explorers such as Christopher Columbus, Vasco da Gama, and Ferdinand Magellan embarked on journeys that would forever alter the course of history. These explorations were not just about finding new trade routes; they were about asserting dominance over newly discovered territories and their peoples.

The encounter between the Old World and the New World was brutal and transformative. The indigenous populations of the

Americas, Africa, and Asia were subjected to a form of exploitation and subjugation that was unprecedented in its scope and intensity. The arrival of Europeans brought about the collapse of entire civilizations, such as the Aztec and Inca Empires in the Americas, and led to the enslavement of millions of people in Africa. The transatlantic slave trade, which saw the forced migration of Africans to the Americas, is one of the darkest chapters in human history, driven by the Western desire for economic gain.

As European powers established colonies in the Americas, Africa, and Asia, they implemented systems of governance and economic exploitation designed to benefit the colonizers at the expense of the colonized. The wealth extracted from these colonies fueled the growth of European economies and financed the expansion of their empires. The colonizers justified their actions through a belief in their own superiority, a belief that was often couched in religious and cultural terms. The spread of Christianity was used as a pretext for conquest, with missionaries often playing a dual role as both spiritual guides and agents of colonial expansion.

The Industrial Revolution, which began in Britain in the late 18th century, further solidified Western dominance. The technological advancements of this period, such as the steam engine, the spinning jenny, and the power loom, revolutionized production processes and led to the mass production of goods. These developments gave Western nations a significant economic advantage over the rest of the world, allowing them to dominate global trade and industry. The rise of industrial capitalism also fueled the expansion of European empires, as colonizers sought new markets for their goods and new sources of raw materials.

The 19th century was marked by the "Scramble for Africa," a period of intense competition among European powers to colonize and control as much of Africa as possible. This period of imperialism was driven by a combination of economic interests, strategic considerations, and a belief in the civilizing mission of the West. The Berlin Conference of 1884-1885, in which European powers carved up Africa without any regard for the interests or wishes of the African people, is a stark example of the ruthlessness with which Western hegemony was established. The boundaries drawn by the colonizers have had lasting impacts on the political and social structures of African nations, contributing to conflicts and instability that persist to this day.

The two World Wars of the 20th century, while devastating in their impact on Europe, also served to consolidate Western dominance on a global scale. The Treaty of Versailles, which ended World War I, established a new international order centered around the League of Nations, an institution dominated by Western powers. The post-World War II period saw the emergence of the United States and the Soviet Union as superpowers, with the U.S. taking on the role of the leader of the "free world." The establishment of the United Nations, the Bretton Woods institutions (the International Monetary Fund and the World Bank), and other international bodies further entrenched Western influence in global affairs.

The Cold War era was characterized by a global struggle for influence between the United States and the Soviet Union, with much of the non-Western world caught in the middle. The U.S. and its allies justified their interventions in countries such as Korea, Vietnam, and Afghanistan as necessary to contain the spread of communism. However, these interventions often resulted in prolonged conflicts, human suffering, and the destabilization of entire regions. The legacy of these conflicts continues to shape global politics, with many of the challenges faced by countries in Asia, Africa, and Latin America today rooted in the actions of Western powers during the Cold War.

In the post-Cold War era, the collapse of the Soviet Union and the rise of globalization ushered in a new phase of Western dominance. The United States, as the sole remaining superpower, sought to promote a global order based on liberal democracy and free-market capitalism. This new world order was characterized by the spread of Western values and institutions, often through economic pressure, diplomatic influence, and, in some cases, military intervention. The promise of globalization was one of economic growth, cultural exchange, and the spread of democracy. However, the reality has been more complex, with many countries experiencing increased inequality, social unrest, and the erosion of traditional cultures.

The financial crises of the late 20th and early 21st centuries, particularly the 2008 global financial crisis, exposed the vulnerabilities of the global economic system and the limits of Western economic models. The crisis, which originated in the United States, had a ripple effect across the world, leading to economic downturns, unemployment, and social unrest in many countries. The response to the crisis, characterized by austerity measures and bailouts for financial institutions, further highlighted the disparities in power and influence between the West and the rest of the world. The promises of economic stability and prosperity, which had been central to the Western model of globalization, were called into question as millions of people around the world faced economic hardship.

The impact of Western hegemony is also evident in the realm of culture and ideology. The spread of Western media, entertainment, and consumer culture has led to the homogenization of cultures around the world, with traditional practices and beliefs increasingly being replaced by Western norms. This cultural imperialism has been both subtle and pervasive, influencing everything from fashion and food to language and values. The dominance of English as the global lingua franca, the popularity of Hollywood films, and the proliferation of Western brands are all examples of the ways in which Western culture has permeated global society. However, this cultural dominance has also led to resistance and a reassertion of local identities, as people around the world seek to preserve their cultural heritage in the face of globalization.

As we move further into the 21st century, the legacy of Western hegemony continues to shape global politics, economics, and culture. The rise of new powers such as China and India, the resurgence of nationalism and populism in the West, and the growing awareness of the environmental and social costs of globalization all point to a world in transition. The promises made by the West—of democracy, development, and cultural progress—are increasingly being challenged by the realities of a world that is more interconnected, yet more divided, than ever before.

The story of Western hegemony is not just a story of power and control, but also a story of broken promises. From the promises of civilization and development made to the colonized peoples of Africa, Asia, and the Americas, to the promises of democracy and freedom made during the Cold War, to the promises of prosperity and progress made in the era of globalization, the gap between what was promised and what was delivered is stark. The consequences of these broken promises are still being felt today, as nations and peoples grapple with the legacies of colonization, imperialism, and globalization.

Chapter 2: Imperialism and the Scramble for Africa

The Scramble for Africa stands as one of the most vivid examples of Western imperialism's brutal and far-reaching impact. It was a period characterized by an aggressive race among European powers to conquer and colonize as much of Africa as possible, driven by a combination of economic, political, and ideological motivations. This chapter will explore the origins, execution, and enduring consequences of the Scramble for Africa, delving into the complex web of interests and actions that led to the colonization of an entire continent.

The roots of the Scramble for Africa can be traced back to the economic and political changes occurring in Europe during the late 19th century. The Industrial Revolution had dramatically transformed European economies, leading to increased production capacities and a growing demand for raw materials. Europe's industrialized nations, particularly Britain, France, and Germany, sought new sources of raw materials to feed their factories and new markets in which to sell their manufactured goods. Africa, with its vast natural resources and relatively untapped markets, became a prime target for European expansion.

Economic motivations, however, were not the only driving force behind the Scramble for Africa. The late 19th century was also a period of intense national rivalry in Europe, as the major powers competed for global influence and prestige. Colonies were seen as symbols of national strength and status, and the acquisition of new territories in Africa was viewed as a way to assert national power on the world stage. This competition was particularly fierce between Britain and France, the two largest colonial powers, but also involved other European nations such as Germany, Belgium, Portugal, and

Italy.

The ideological justification for the Scramble for Africa was rooted in a belief in the superiority of European civilization and the mission to "civilize" the African continent. This belief was often couched in religious terms, with Christian missionaries playing a key role in the colonization process. The spread of Christianity was presented as a moral imperative, with European colonizers claiming to bring the benefits of Western civilization—education, Christianity, and "civilized" governance—to the "backward" peoples of Africa. This paternalistic view, which portrayed African societies as primitive and in need of European guidance, was used to justify the violence and exploitation that accompanied the colonization process.

The Berlin Conference of 1884-1885 was the formal beginning of the Scramble for Africa. Convened by German Chancellor Otto von Bismarck, the conference brought together representatives from 14 European nations to negotiate and formalize the division of Africa among the colonial powers. Notably, no African representatives were present at the conference, and the decisions made there were based entirely on European interests. The resulting agreements set the stage for the rapid colonization of Africa, with European powers carving up the continent into colonies with little regard for the existing ethnic, cultural, or political boundaries.

The colonization of Africa was carried out with brutal efficiency. European powers used a combination of military force, diplomatic pressure, and economic coercion to establish control over African territories. In many cases, African resistance was met with overwhelming force, as European armies, equipped with advanced weaponry, crushed any opposition. The Herero and Namaqua genocide in German South West Africa (modern-day Namibia) is one of the most egregious examples of the violence inflicted on African populations during this period. Between 1904 and 1908, German colonial forces carried out a campaign of extermination against the Herero and Nama peoples, resulting in the deaths of tens of thousands of men, women, and children.

The impact of the Scramble for Africa on the continent was profound and far-reaching. The imposition of European rule disrupted existing political and social structures, leading to the disintegration of traditional kingdoms and empires. The arbitrary borders drawn by the colonizers often grouped together diverse ethnic groups with little in common, sowing the seeds of future conflicts. The exploitation of Africa's natural resources, including minerals, rubber, and agricultural products, was carried out with little regard for the well-being of the African people. Forced labor, land expropriation, and the introduction of cash crop economies left many African communities impoverished and dependent on the colonial economy.

The legacy of the Scramble for Africa is still evident today. The borders drawn by European powers during the colonial period continue to shape the political landscape of Africa, contributing to conflicts and tensions in many regions. The economic exploitation of Africa during the colonial period has had lasting effects on the continent's development, with many African nations struggling to overcome the legacy of underdevelopment and dependence on the global economic system. The social and cultural impact of colonization, including the erosion of traditional practices and the imposition of Western values, continues to be felt in many African societies.

The Scramble for Africa was not just a tragedy for the African people; it was also a significant chapter in the history of Western imperialism. It exemplifies the lengths to which European powers were willing to go in their quest for global dominance, and the devastating impact of that quest on the rest of the world. As we continue to grapple with the legacies of imperialism and colonialism, the story of the Scramble for Africa serves as a powerful reminder of the human cost of Western hegemony.

The political instability in many African countries today can be traced back to the colonial era. The imposition of arbitrary borders, often without regard for existing ethnic or political structures, laid the groundwork for ongoing conflicts. In many cases, colonial rulers manipulated local power dynamics to maintain control, favoring certain groups over others. This legacy of divide-and-rule strategies has contributed to persistent ethnic tensions and conflicts in post-colonial Africa.

The introduction of Western-style governance systems, including centralized bureaucracies and legal frameworks, often did not align with traditional African forms of governance. This mismatch has led to challenges in building effective and legitimate political institutions. In some cases, post-independence leaders, having inherited weak state structures and political institutions from the colonial period, have struggled to establish stable and inclusive governance systems.

The impact of colonialism on political stability is evident in the frequent changes in leadership, military coups, and civil wars that have plagued many African nations. For example, the Democratic Republic of Congo has experienced decades of conflict and instability, partly due to the legacy of colonial exploitation and mismanagement. Similarly, the protracted conflict in South Sudan reflects the complex interplay of colonial legacies and contemporary power struggles.

The economic legacy of colonialism has had a lasting impact on Africa's development trajectory. The colonial economic system was designed to extract resources and generate wealth for European powers, often at the expense of local economies. This system left many African countries with economies heavily dependent on a few primary commodities, such as minerals, agricultural products, and oil.

Post-independence, many African nations found themselves struggling with economic dependency and underdevelopment. The transition from colonial economies to independent economic systems has been fraught with challenges. The lack of diversified economic activities, combined with global market fluctuations and debt crises, has hindered economic growth and development in many African countries.

The legacy of economic exploitation is also evident in the continuing impact of global economic policies. International financial institutions, such as the IMF and the World Bank, have often imposed structural adjustment programs that prioritize debt repayment and market liberalization over social development. These policies have sometimes exacerbated poverty and inequality, reinforcing the economic dependency established during the colonial period.

The cultural impact of colonialism is another area where the legacy of the Scramble for Africa is evident. The imposition of

Western values, languages, and education systems during the colonial period led to the erosion of traditional African cultures and practices. Missionary education and colonial administrations often disregarded local knowledge and customs, promoting Western ideals as superior.

This cultural imperialism has resulted in a complex cultural landscape where traditional African practices coexist with Western influences. The struggle to reclaim and preserve indigenous identities has been a significant aspect of post-colonial cultural revival efforts. African societies have worked to reassert their cultural heritage and adapt traditional practices in the context of a modern globalized world.

The tension between preserving indigenous cultures and adapting to global influences is reflected in various aspects of African life, from language and education to art and media. Efforts to promote and celebrate African cultural heritage, such as the revival of traditional arts and the promotion of indigenous languages, are part of a broader movement to reclaim and preserve African identities.

The international response to the legacy of the Scramble for Africa has been multifaceted. On one hand, there has been a growing recognition of the need to address historical injustices and support African development. Various international organizations, NGOs, and aid programs have sought to address some of the economic and social challenges facing African countries. Initiatives aimed at promoting fair trade, supporting sustainable development, and addressing climate change are part of a broader effort to mitigate the effects of colonialism.

However, the continued dominance of Western powers and global economic systems often perpetuates inequalities and undermines efforts to achieve meaningful development. The global economic order, characterized by trade imbalances, debt crises, and uneven development, reflects the ongoing influence of colonial-era structures. Efforts to reform international financial institutions and promote equitable development are essential to addressing these persistent challenges.

The challenges of addressing the legacy of colonialism are

compounded by the complex and evolving nature of global power dynamics. As new powers, such as China and India, emerge on the global stage, the dynamics of international relations and development are shifting. The role of these emerging powers in Africa, both as partners and competitors to Western nations, will shape the future trajectory of the continent.

Despite the profound impacts of colonialism, African societies have demonstrated remarkable resilience and agency. The ability to adapt, preserve, and transform cultural practices in the face of external pressures is a testament to the strength and adaptability of African peoples. Efforts to build new political and economic systems, promote social justice, and reclaim cultural heritage reflect the ongoing dynamism and creativity of African societies.

Post-colonial Africa has seen significant achievements in various areas,including economic development, political stability, and cultural revival. The emergence of new leaders, movements, and institutions reflects a commitment to overcoming the challenges of the colonial past and building a more equitable future. As African nations continue to navigate the complexities of global politics and economics, their ability to assert their agency and shape their own destinies remains a key factor in the continent's development.

In terms of political achievements, several African countries have made strides in establishing more democratic and inclusive governance systems. Nations such as Ghana and Botswana have garnered international praise for their stable democracies and effective governance, showcasing the potential for positive change in post-colonial Africa. These successes highlight the ability of African nations to overcome the legacies of colonialism and build resilient political institutions.

Economic development has also seen notable progress in various parts of Africa. Countries like Kenya and Nigeria have experienced periods of rapid economic growth, driven by sectors such as technology and natural resources. The rise of vibrant entrepreneurial ecosystems and the growth of industries such as fintech and renewable energy demonstrate the continent's potential to leverage its resources and human capital for sustainable development.

Cultural revival is another area where African societies have made significant strides. There has been a resurgence of interest in traditional arts, languages, and customs, as well as a growing appreciation for African heritage on the global stage. The promotion of African literature, music, and film has gained international recognition, contributing to a broader understanding and appreciation of African cultures. This cultural renaissance reflects the continent's ongoing efforts to reclaim and celebrate its diverse heritage.

Nevertheless, the journey towards overcoming the impacts of colonialism is far from complete. Many African countries still grapple with the consequences of historical exploitation, including persistent economic challenges and political instability. Addressing these issues requires continued efforts to build robust institutions, promote equitable economic policies, and support cultural and social development.

The global community also has a role to play in addressing the legacies of colonialism. International cooperation and support for African development initiatives can help to mitigate the ongoing effects of historical injustices. Efforts to promote fair trade, support sustainable development, and address global inequalities are essential for creating a more just and equitable world.

As we move forward, it is important to recognize the complexities of Africa's post-colonial experience and the diverse ways in which the continent is responding to its historical legacies. By acknowledging and addressing the multifaceted impacts of colonialism, we can contribute to a more nuanced understanding of the challenges and opportunities facing African nations today.

The story of the Scramble for Africa is not just a historical account but a lens through which we can view the ongoing dynamics of global power and influence. It serves as a reminder of the human cost of imperialism and the enduring impact of colonial legacies on the world. As we continue to explore the broader implications of Western hegemony, the lessons from Africa's experience can inform efforts to build a more equitable and inclusive global future.

The legacy of the Scramble for Africa extends beyond the political and economic realms and profoundly affects social and cultural dimensions as well. The imposition of European values and systems on African societies led to significant disruptions in social structures and cultural practices. Traditional systems of governance, social organization, and cultural practices were often dismissed or actively suppressed in favor of Western models.

Socially, colonialism introduced new class hierarchies and divisions. The colonial administration often created or exacerbated social stratification by favoring certain ethnic or social groups over others. This manipulation of social hierarchies contributed to long-standing tensions and conflicts within many African societies. The division of people into categories based on colonial administrative needs, rather than traditional social organization, has had lasting repercussions. In countries like Nigeria, the colonial practice of favoring certain ethnic groups for administrative roles has led to enduring ethnic conflicts and power struggles.

Culturally, the impact of colonialism was profound. European colonizers often dismissed or belittled African cultures and practices, viewing them through a lens of superiority. This led to the erosion of traditional cultural practices and languages, as colonial education systems and missionary work promoted European values and norms. Many indigenous languages were suppressed, and traditional arts and customs were either marginalized or redefined through the lens of European standards. This cultural suppression has led to ongoing efforts to reclaim and revive African heritage, with a growing emphasis on preserving traditional languages, arts, and practices.

In terms of education, the colonial system imposed Western curricula and teaching methods, often disregarding or devaluing indigenous knowledge. The introduction of European educational models aimed to create a class of educated Africans who could assist in administering the colonies, but it often failed to address the broader educational needs of African societies. The legacy of this educational system is evident in many African countries, where colonial-era curricula continue to influence educational practices and priorities. Efforts to reform education systems to better reflect and integrate indigenous knowledge and practices are ongoing, but challenges remain.

The economic legacy of colonialism is also evident in the uneven development of infrastructure and industry across the continent. The colonial focus on resource extraction and export-oriented economies left many African countries with underdeveloped infrastructure and limited industrial capacity. While some countries have made progress in developing their economies, others continue to struggle with the constraints imposed by colonial-era economic structures. The reliance on primary commodity exports and the lack of diversified industrial development have contributed to economic vulnerability and dependence on global markets.

In recent years, there has been a growing recognition of the need to address these historical injustices and support African development. International organizations, non-governmental organizations, and African governments themselves are working to promote economic development, improve governance, and support cultural revival. Initiatives aimed at promoting fair trade, supporting sustainable development, and addressing global inequalities are part of a broader effort to address the legacies of colonialism.

The emergence of new global powers, such as China and India, has also added a new dimension to the dynamics of international relations in Africa. These countries are engaging with African nations in ways that both challenge and complement Western influence. The growing presence of China in Africa, for example, has led to increased investment in infrastructure and development projects, but it also raises questions about the potential for new forms of exploitation and dependency. The involvement of these new actors highlights the shifting nature of global power and the need for a more nuanced understanding of contemporary international relations.

As African nations continue to navigate their post-colonial realities, the ability to assert their agency and shape their own destinies remains a crucial factor. The resilience and creativity of African societies in the face of historical challenges are evident in various aspects of contemporary life, from political and economic development to cultural revival. The ongoing efforts to address the legacies of colonialism and build a more equitable future reflect the dynamic and evolving nature of Africa's journey.

The story of Africa's post-colonial experience is a testament to the enduring impact of Western hegemony and the complex interplay of historical legacies and contemporary challenges. It underscores the need for a comprehensive understanding of the past and its implications for the present and future. By acknowledging and addressing the multifaceted impacts of colonialism, we can contribute to a more informed and equitable global dialogue.

The legacy of the Scramble for Africa serves as a powerful reminder of the consequences of imperialism and the importance of addressing historical injustices. As we look to the future, the lessons from Africa's experience can guide efforts to build a more just and inclusive world. The ongoing efforts to reclaim and preserve cultural heritage, promote economic development, and address the impacts of colonialism reflect the resilience and determination of African societies to shape their own destinies and contribute to a more equitable global community.

Chapter 3: The Cold War and Western Interventions

The Cold War era, spanning from the end of World War II to the early 1990s, was characterized by intense geopolitical rivalry between the United States and the Soviet Union. This period not only shaped the global balance of power but also had significant implications for various regions, particularly Africa, Latin America, and the Middle East. The interplay of superpower interests during this time led to a series of interventions and conflicts that have had lasting effects on global politics and regional stability.

In the aftermath of World War II, African nations began to gain independence from European colonial powers, entering a new phase of geopolitical contestation. The Cold War presented African leaders with a complex array of choices as they navigated their newfound sovereignty. Both the United States and the Soviet Union sought to expand their influence on the continent, often through support for different political factions or regimes.

One illustrative case of Cold War intervention in Africa was the Congo Crisis. Following the Congo's independence in 1960, the political landscape quickly became a battleground for Cold War interests. Patrice Lumumba, the country's first Prime Minister, sought to establish a strong, independent Congo. His alignment with socialist ideals and opposition to Western influence drew the ire of the U.S. and its allies. The CIA and Belgian operatives were involved in efforts to undermine Lumumba's government, culminating in his assassination in 1961. This intervention not only destabilized the Congo but also set a precedent for future Western involvement in African politics, where geopolitical interests often took precedence over local stability and development.

In subsequent decades, Africa witnessed numerous other interventions. The support for various authoritarian regimes in exchange for alignment with Western or Soviet interests frequently resulted in long-term instability. The U.S. supported leaders like Mobutu Sese Seko in Zaire (now the Democratic Republic of the Congo), whose corrupt regime contributed to the country's ongoing struggles. Similarly, the Soviet Union's support for Marxist regimes in Southern Africa, such as those in Angola and Mozambique, often intensified regional conflicts.

Latin America was another critical arena of Cold War rivalry, where the ideological struggle between capitalism and communism played out through high-stakes interventions. The Cuban Revolution of 1959, led by Fidel Castro and Che Guevara, significantly altered the geopolitical landscape of the region. The establishment of a communist government in Cuba was perceived as a direct challenge to U.S. interests in the Western Hemisphere.

The U.S. response to the Cuban Revolution included a range of interventions aimed at undermining Castro's regime. The most infamous was the Bay of Pigs invasion in 1961, orchestrated by the CIA, which ended in a humiliating defeat for the U.S. The failure of this operation only served to consolidate Castro's position and push Cuba closer to the Soviet Union. The Cuban Missile Crisis of 1962 further escalated tensions, bringing the world to the brink of nuclear war.

In response to the perceived threat of communism spreading in Latin America, the U.S. adopted a policy of supporting anti-communist regimes and military coups. The 1973 coup in Chile, which overthrew President Salvador Allende, is a stark example. The U.S. provided support to General Augusto Pinochet's military regime, which implemented a brutal and repressive dictatorship. Pinochet's regime was marked by widespread human rights abuses, including torture, disappearances, and executions. The U.S. support for such regimes reflected the prioritization of ideological alignment over democratic principles and human rights.

The Middle East was another region significantly affected by Cold War interventions. The strategic importance of the region, with its vast oil reserves and geopolitical significance, made it a focal point for both superpowers. The U.S. and its allies sought to bolster friendly regimes and counter Soviet influence, while the Soviet Union aimed to support Arab states and revolutionary movements.

The U.S. support for Israel was a central element of its Middle Eastern strategy. Following the establishment of Israel in 1948, the U.S. provided extensive military and economic aid, reinforcing its ability to confront its Arab neighbors. This support played a crucial role in shaping the dynamics of the Arab-Israeli conflicts, including the Six-Day War of 1967 and the Yom Kippur War of 1973. The U.S.'s alignment with Israel contributed to regional tensions and ongoing conflicts that persist to this day.

Conversely, the Soviet Union extended support to Arab states such as Egypt, Syria, and Iraq. The Soviet Union provided military aid and political support in their conflicts with Israel. The Soviet involvement in regional disputes, including the 1973 Yom Kippur War, was part of a broader strategy to counter U.S. influence and assert Soviet power in the Middle East.

The Cold War also saw various proxy conflicts in the region, such as the Iranian Revolution of 1979. The U.S. had previously supported the Shah of Iran, whose regime was overthrown by revolutionary forces led by Ayatollah Khomeini. The rise of the Islamic Republic of Iran, with its anti-Western stance, altered the regional balance of power and led to strained relations between Iran and the U.S. The revolution's aftermath, including the Iran-Iraq War of the 1980s, was marked by further intervention and shifting alliances.

Covert operations and intelligence activities were a significant feature of Cold War strategies. Both the U.S. and the Soviet Union relied on espionage, propaganda, and covert actions to advance their strategic interests. Intelligence agencies such as the CIA and the KGB played pivotal roles in shaping political outcomes and influencing public perceptions.

Covert operations often involved supporting political factions, conducting sabotage, and engaging in psychological warfare. The use of covert tactics allowed superpowers to exert influence while avoiding direct confrontation. However, these operations frequently had unintended consequences and contributed to political instability in various regions.

One notable example was the CIA's involvement in the 1953 coup in Iran. The CIA orchestrated the overthrow of Prime Minister Mohammad Mossadegh, who had nationalized the country's oil industry. The coup, known as Operation Ajax, reinstated the Shah of Iran and secured Western interests in Iranian oil. The intervention had long-term repercussions, including the strengthening of the Shah's repressive regime and the eventual rise of the Islamic Republic.

Similarly, the Soviet Union engaged in covert activities to support socialist and revolutionary movements worldwide. Soviet support for leftist groups and regimes was part of a broader strategy to counter Western influence and promote communism. The consequences of these interventions often included prolonged conflicts and political instability in the affected regions.

The legacy of Cold War interventions is evident in the political, social, and economic challenges faced by many regions today. The imposition of external interests and the manipulation of local politics during the Cold War created long-lasting effects that continue to shape global affairs.

In Africa, the legacy of Cold War interventions is reflected in ongoing political instability, ethnic conflicts, and challenges in governance. The support for authoritarian regimes and the undermining of democratic processes have left a lasting impact on the continent's political landscape. Efforts to address these issues and build democratic institutions are ongoing, but the historical legacy of Cold War interventions remains a significant challenge.

In Latin America, the Cold War era left a legacy of political repression, human rights abuses, and social divisions. The support for military dictatorships and the undermining of democratic processes have had enduring consequences for the region's political and social development. The pursuit of justice, reconciliation, and democratic governance continues to be a priority for many Latin American countries.

In the Middle East, the impact of Cold War interventions is evident in the ongoing regional conflicts and geopolitical tensions. The legacy of superpower rivalry and the support for opposing sides in regional disputes have contributed to the protracted nature of conflicts and the difficulties in achieving lasting peace and stability.

The Cold War also highlighted the ethical and strategic complexities of covert operations and intelligence activities. The use of espionage and covert tactics raised important questions about the balance between national security and individual rights. The lessons learned from Cold War interventions emphasize the need for a more nuanced approach to international relations and the importance of addressing the long-term consequences of external interventions.

As the world moves forward, it is essential to acknowledge and address the legacy of Cold War interventions. By understanding the complexities of past actions and their impact on global affairs, we can work towards building a more just and equitable international system. The lessons from the Cold War era can guide efforts to address contemporary challenges and promote a more inclusive and peaceful global order.

The Cold War and Western interventions had a profound and far-reaching impact on various regions of the world. The legacy of these interventions is evident in the political instability, social divisions, and ongoing conflicts that continue to shape global affairs. By acknowledging and addressing the consequences of Cold War dynamics, we can work towards building a more just and equitable world, where the lessons of the past inform our efforts to address the challenges of the present and future.

Chapter 4: The Rise of Globalization and Its Discontents

The end of the Cold War marked the beginning of a new era in global politics and economics. The dissolution of the Soviet Union and the triumph of capitalist democracies ushered in a period characterized by rapid globalization, economic integration, and the spread of neoliberal policies. While this new global order promised unprecedented economic growth and connectivity, it also generated significant discontents and inequalities. This chapter explores the rise of globalization, the principles behind neoliberalism, and the consequences that have unfolded in various regions of the world.

Globalization, driven by advancements in technology, communication, and transportation, facilitated unprecedented levels of economic integration. The collapse of trade barriers, the expansion of international trade, and the growth of multinational corporations created a highly interconnected global economy. The promise of globalization was that it would lead to greater prosperity, economic efficiency, and cultural exchange.

The neoliberal policies that accompanied globalization emphasized deregulation, privatization, and the reduction of state intervention in the economy. Proponents of neoliberalism argued that free markets would lead to more efficient allocation of resources, stimulate economic growth, and promote individual freedom. The Washington Consensus, which outlined a set of economic policies including fiscal discipline, market liberalization, and trade openness, became the guiding framework for many countries transitioning to market economies.

In practice, the effects of neoliberal policies have been mixed. While some countries experienced significant economic growth and development, others faced severe social and economic consequences. The disparity between the benefits of globalization for different regions has highlighted the unequal distribution of its rewards and challenges.

In the developing world, the impact of globalization has been particularly pronounced. Countries that embraced neoliberal reforms often experienced short-term economic growth but faced long-term challenges related to income inequality and social instability. The privatization of state-owned enterprises, for example, frequently led to job losses and reduced access to essential services for the most vulnerable populations. The reduction of trade barriers exposed local industries to global competition, which sometimes resulted in the collapse of domestic businesses and the erosion of local economies.

In Latin America, the 1980s and 1990s were marked by a series of neoliberal reforms implemented under the guidance of international financial institutions such as the International Monetary Fund (IMF) and the World Bank. The region's embrace of market-oriented policies led to economic liberalization, including trade deregulation and privatization of public utilities. While these policies were intended to stimulate economic growth, they often exacerbated social inequalities and contributed to economic instability.

In countries like Argentina and Brazil, the implementation of neoliberal policies resulted in significant social upheaval. The privatization of state-owned companies led to job losses and reduced access to public services. Economic crises, such as the Argentine financial crisis of 2001, highlighted the vulnerabilities associated with rapid economic liberalization and the shortcomings of neoliberal approaches.

Similarly, in Africa, the adoption of neoliberal policies in the 1990s was promoted as a means of fostering economic development and reducing poverty. However, the consequences of these policies were often detrimental to the continent's most vulnerable populations. The imposition of structural adjustment programs by international financial institutions required governments to implement austerity measures, including cuts to social spending and subsidies. These measures often led to increased poverty, reduced access to healthcare and education, and social unrest.

The effects of globalization were not confined to the developing world. In advanced economies, the shift towards neoliberal policies also produced significant challenges. The emphasis on free markets and deregulation contributed to the rise of financialization and income inequality. The 2008 global financial crisis, which originated in the financial markets of advanced economies, exposed the vulnerabilities of the neoliberal economic model and the risks associated with unregulated financial practices.

The crisis highlighted the interconnectedness of the global economy and the potential for economic shocks to spread rapidly across borders. The aftermath of the crisis led to widespread economic hardship, including job losses, foreclosures, and reduced economic growth. The response to the crisis, which included government bailouts of financial institutions and stimulus measures, sparked debates about the role of state intervention in managing economic instability.

Globalization has also had cultural and social implications. The spread of global media, consumer products, and cultural influences has transformed societies around the world. While globalization has facilitated greater cultural exchange and access to information, it has also raised concerns about cultural homogenization and the erosion of local traditions. The dominance of Western media and entertainment has been criticized for overshadowing local cultures and contributing to the loss of cultural diversity.

The impact of globalization on labor markets has been another area of concern. The shift towards global supply chains and the pursuit of lower production costs have led to the outsourcing of jobs and the exploitation of labor in developing countries. Workers in low-wage economies often face poor working conditions, low wages, and limited labor rights. The race to the bottom in labor standards has raised ethical questions about the treatment of workers and the responsibilities of multinational corporations.

In response to the discontents associated with globalization, there has been a rise in populist and anti-globalization movements. These movements, which have gained prominence in various countries, criticize the negative effects of globalization on local economies, communities, and national sovereignty. Populist leaders often argue that globalization has favored elites and multinational corporations at the expense of ordinary citizens. They advocate for protectionist policies, trade barriers, and a reevaluation of international agreements.

The backlash against globalization has manifested in different ways, including the rise of nationalist political movements, increased skepticism towards international institutions, and calls for greater economic protectionism. In some cases, the anti-globalization sentiment has led to political upheaval and the election of leaders who challenge the established global order.

The response to globalization's challenges requires a nuanced approach that addresses the needs of both developed and developing countries. Efforts to reform the global economic system and promote more inclusive and equitable growth are essential. This includes addressing income inequality, enhancing labor rights, and ensuring that the benefits of globalization are more broadly shared.

One potential avenue for addressing the challenges of globalization is through the promotion of sustainable development. The pursuit of sustainable development goals, including reducing poverty, addressing climate change, and promoting social inclusion, offers a framework for creating a more equitable and resilient global economy. By prioritizing sustainability and social justice, policymakers can work towards mitigating the negative impacts of globalization and ensuring that its benefits are more evenly distributed.

The experience of different countries in navigating the complexities of globalization provides valuable lessons for shaping future policies. While globalization has brought significant opportunities and advancements, it has also exposed vulnerabilities and inequalities. The challenge is to strike a balance between leveraging the benefits of globalization and addressing its shortcomings.

As globalization deepened, the shift towards a knowledge-based economy emerged as another significant transformation. The rise of technology and digital innovation brought about new opportunities and challenges, reshaping industries and labor markets. The information revolution, characterized by rapid advancements in computing and communication technologies, has accelerated the pace of globalization and altered the nature of economic activity.

The digital age has facilitated the growth of global networks and the dissemination of information on an unprecedented scale. The internet and digital platforms have enabled businesses to reach global markets, connect with consumers, and collaborate across borders. The rise of e-commerce and digital services has created new economic opportunities and disrupted traditional business models.

However, the digital divide has highlighted the unequal distribution of technological benefits. While some regions and individuals have been able to leverage digital technologies for economic and social advancement, others have been left behind. Access to technology, internet connectivity, and digital literacy remain significant barriers for many in developing countries. This digital inequality exacerbates existing disparities and raises questions about the inclusivity of the global digital economy.

The impact of technological change extends beyond the economy to social and cultural realms. Social media platforms, for example, have transformed how people communicate, share information, and engage with global communities. The rise of social media has given voice to marginalized groups and facilitated grassroots movements for social change. At the same time, it has also been a platform for misinformation, polarization, and manipulation, raising concerns about the quality of information and its impact on public discourse.

The influence of technology on labor markets is another area of concern. Automation and artificial intelligence (AI) have the potential to transform industries and increase productivity, but they also pose risks to employment. The displacement of workers due to technological advancements has led to concerns about job security and the future of work. The need for reskilling and upskilling has become a critical issue as workers seek to adapt to the changing demands of the labor market.

In the context of globalization, the interaction between technology and labor markets has amplified the challenges of economic inequality. While technology has created new opportunities for innovation and growth, it has also contributed to wage stagnation and job polarization. The benefits of technological advancements have not been evenly distributed, leading to increased economic disparities within and between countries.

The environmental impact of globalization and technological progress is another pressing issue. The pursuit of economic growth and consumption has contributed to environmental degradation, climate change, and resource depletion. The global economy's reliance on fossil fuels, deforestation, and industrialization has had significant consequences for the planet's ecosystems and climate. Addressing these environmental challenges requires a global effort to promote sustainable practices and transition to a low-carbon economy.

Efforts to address the environmental impact of globalization include international agreements and initiatives aimed at promoting sustainability and reducing carbon emissions. The Paris Agreement, for example, represents a global commitment to combat climate change and limit global temperature rise. However, the effectiveness of these efforts depends on the willingness of countries to adhere to their commitments and implement meaningful policies.

In addition to environmental concerns, the cultural impact of globalization has sparked debates about cultural homogenization and the preservation of local traditions. The dominance of Western media and cultural products has raised questions about the erosion of cultural diversity and the influence of global consumer culture. While globalization has facilitated cultural exchange and increased access to diverse perspectives, it has also led to the spread of a homogenized global culture that sometimes overshadows local traditions and values.

The challenges of globalization are further complicated by geopolitical dynamics and shifting power relations. The rise of emerging economies, such as China and India, has altered the global balance of power and introduced new complexities to international relations. The emergence of China as a global economic powerhouse has led to increased competition and tension with established Western powers. The strategic and economic interests of major powers often intersect with global economic and social issues, influencing the direction of globalization and its consequences.

In response to these challenges, there has been growing advocacy for more inclusive and equitable approaches to globalization. Efforts to address economic inequality, promote sustainable development, and enhance social protections are critical for creating a more balanced and just global system. The promotion of fair trade practices, support for local economies, and investment in social infrastructure can help mitigate some of the negative impacts of globalization and ensure that its benefits are more widely shared.

The role of international institutions and governance in managing globalization is also crucial. Organizations such as the United Nations, the World Trade Organization, and regional development banks play a key role in shaping global economic policies and addressing global challenges. Strengthening international cooperation and ensuring that these institutions are responsive to the needs of all countries can help promote a more equitable and sustainable global order.

The future of globalization will depend on how these challenges are addressed and the ability of countries and international institutions to navigate the complexities of a rapidly changing world. The lessons learned from past experiences and the ongoing efforts to address the shortcomings of globalization will shape the trajectory of global economic and social development.

In conclusion, the rise of globalization has brought about significant economic, social, and cultural transformations. While it has created opportunities for growth and connectivity, it has also generated discontents and inequalities. The challenges associated with globalization highlight the need for a more inclusive and sustainable approach to global development. By addressing these challenges and working towards a more equitable global system, we can ensure that the benefits of globalization are shared more broadly and that its negative impacts are mitigated.

Chapter 5: The Impact of Western Hegemony on Global Trade and Economic Policies

The concept of Western hegemony in global trade and economic policies refers to the influence exerted by Western nations, particularly the United States and European countries, over international economic systems and trade practices. This influence has shaped the development of global trade norms, economic policies, and international financial institutions. The repercussions of this hegemony are felt across various regions and sectors, revealing both benefits and significant challenges for countries around the world.

The foundation of Western economic dominance can be traced back to the post-World War II era, when the Bretton Woods Conference established the international financial system that favored Western economic interests. The International Monetary Fund (IMF) and the World Bank were created to provide financial stability and support economic development, but their policies often reflected the priorities and perspectives of their Western founders. This framework established a global economic order in which Western countries held significant influence over global trade and economic policies.

Trade liberalization became a central tenet of Western economic policy, promoting the reduction of trade barriers and the expansion of global markets. The General Agreement on Tariffs and Trade

(GATT), which later evolved into the World Trade Organization (WTO), embodied these principles. While the liberalization of trade facilitated economic growth and integration, it also introduced challenges for developing countries. Many countries struggled to compete in an increasingly open market, facing obstacles such as limited access to technology, capital, and skilled labor.

The policies promoted by Western-dominated institutions often emphasized market-driven reforms and structural adjustments. In many developing countries, these reforms were implemented as conditions for receiving financial assistance from the IMF or World Bank. While the intention was to promote economic stability and growth, the results were frequently mixed. Structural adjustment programs, which included measures such as privatization, deregulation, and austerity, often led to economic instability and social unrest. The emphasis on market liberalization sometimes exacerbated existing inequalities and undermined local economies.

The impact of Western economic policies on global trade is evident in various sectors, including agriculture, manufacturing, and services. In the agricultural sector, subsidies provided by Western countries to their domestic farmers have distorted global markets. These subsidies often result in overproduction and lower prices for agricultural products, which can undermine the competitiveness of farmers in developing countries. The imbalance in global agricultural trade has significant implications for food security and rural development in poorer regions.

In the manufacturing sector, the globalization of supply chains has led to the outsourcing of production to countries with lower labor costs. While this has created economic opportunities in some developing countries, it has also raised concerns about labor conditions and environmental sustainability. The pursuit of cost-cutting measures often results in poor working conditions, low wages, and limited labor rights for workers in developing countries. The environmental impact of manufacturing practices, including pollution and resource depletion, is another significant concern.

The services sector has also been affected by Western economic policies, particularly through the expansion of financial services and the liberalization of trade in services. The growth of global financial markets and the dominance of Western financial institutions have introduced new dynamics to the global economy. The proliferation of financial products and services, including derivatives and speculative investments, has contributed to financial instability and economic crises.

The influence of Western hegemony extends to the realm of intellectual property rights. The enforcement of intellectual property laws, driven by Western countries and multinational corporations, has significant implications for innovation and access to technology. While intellectual property protection is intended to encourage innovation, it can also create barriers to accessing essential technologies and medicines, particularly in developing countries. The high costs associated with patented technologies and pharmaceuticals can limit access to life-saving treatments and hinder technological advancement.

The geopolitical dimensions of Western hegemony are also evident in the context of trade agreements and economic diplomacy. Western countries have leveraged their economic power to shape trade agreements and influence global economic policies. Bilateral and multilateral trade agreements often reflect the interests of Western nations and may impose conditions that favor their economic priorities. These agreements can have far-reaching consequences for trade relations, economic development, and sovereignty.

The impact of Western economic policies is not limited to developing countries. Advanced economies have also experienced the effects of global economic integration and the influence of Western-dominated institutions. The 2008 global financial crisis, which originated in Western financial markets, demonstrated the interconnectedness of the global economy and the vulnerabilities associated with financial liberalization. The crisis highlighted the risks of unregulated financial practices and the need for greater oversight and regulation of financial markets.

In response to the challenges posed by Western hegemony and global economic policies, there have been efforts to reform international economic institutions and promote more equitable practices. Calls for reform of the IMF and World Bank have focused on increasing the representation of developing countries and ensuring that their needs and perspectives are better reflected in decision-making processes. Efforts to address trade imbalances, promote fair trade practices, and enhance labor rights are also part of the broader push for a more inclusive and just global economic system.

Regional economic arrangements and alternative economic models have emerged as responses to Western-dominated frameworks. The rise of regional trade agreements, such as the African Continental Free Trade Area (AfCFTA) and the Comprehensive and Progressive Agreement for Trans-Pacific Partnership (CPTPP), reflects efforts to enhance regional economic integration and reduce reliance on Western-dominated trade systems. These arrangements aim to create new opportunities for economic cooperation and development while addressing some of the limitations of existing global trade structures.

The exploration of alternative economic models, including those that emphasize sustainability, social equity, and local development, provides additional avenues for addressing the challenges of Western hegemony. Concepts such as de-growth, social entrepreneurship, and sustainable development offer frameworks for rethinking economic policies and practices in ways that prioritize the well-being of people and the planet.

The consequences of Western hegemony in global trade and economic policies also manifest in the realm of development assistance and foreign aid. Western countries and international institutions have historically been major providers of development aid, often with the intention of supporting economic growth and poverty reduction in developing countries. However, the manner in which aid is distributed and the conditions attached to it have significant implications for the recipient countries.

Development aid has often been tied to the implementation of specific economic policies or structural reforms dictated by Western donors. These conditions, which might include requirements for liberalization, privatization, or fiscal austerity, are intended to ensure that aid is used effectively and that recipient countries adopt practices that align with Western economic models. However, these conditions can sometimes exacerbate existing vulnerabilities and create additional challenges for developing countries.

For instance, the imposition of austerity measures as a condition for receiving aid can lead to cuts in essential public services and social programs, affecting the most vulnerable populations. Similarly, the push for privatization can result in the transfer of public assets to private entities, often without adequate regulatory oversight. This can lead to increased inequality and reduced access to essential services for low-income communities.

The impact of foreign aid is further complicated by issues of governance and corruption. In some cases, aid can inadvertently support corrupt practices or reinforce existing power structures, undermining efforts to promote genuine development and reform. Ensuring that aid is used effectively and reaches those who need it most requires robust mechanisms for transparency, accountability, and local participation.

The geopolitical motivations behind development assistance also play a role in shaping its impact. Aid can be used as a tool for advancing strategic interests, such as securing political alliances or accessing natural resources. This can lead to the prioritization of certain countries or regions over others, based on their strategic value rather than their development needs. The alignment of aid with geopolitical objectives can also create dependencies and undermine the autonomy of recipient countries.

In addition to development aid, the influence of Western hegemony extends to global financial markets and investment flows. The dominance of Western financial institutions and multinational corporations has significant implications for global economic dynamics. Investment decisions made by these entities can impact economic growth, employment, and environmental sustainability in various regions.

The pursuit of profit and shareholder value by multinational corporations often drives investment decisions, which may not always align with the development goals of host countries. For example, large-scale infrastructure projects or resource extraction operations can have significant social and environmental impacts, including displacement of communities, environmental degradation, and labor exploitation. Ensuring that investment practices are conducted responsibly and with respect for local communities and ecosystems is a critical challenge.

The influence of Western financial institutions on global economic policies and regulations also shapes the functioning of financial markets. The dominance of Western financial practices and standards can impact the stability and accessibility of global financial systems. The 2008 financial crisis, for example, highlighted the risks associated with unregulated financial markets and the interconnectedness of global economies. The crisis underscored the need for improved regulatory frameworks and greater oversight of financial practices.

Efforts to address the impact of Western hegemony on global trade and economic policies include initiatives to promote fair trade, enhance labor rights, and improve environmental sustainability. Fair trade practices aim to ensure that producers in developing countries receive equitable compensation for their goods and services, fostering more balanced trade relationships. Enhancing labor rights and improving working conditions for workers in global supply chains are also important steps towards more ethical and sustainable economic practices.

In addition, there is a growing focus on promoting sustainable development and addressing environmental challenges. The integration of environmental considerations into trade and investment policies, as well as the promotion of green technologies and practices, can contribute to a more sustainable and equitable global economy. International agreements, such as the Paris Agreement on climate change, represent collective efforts to address global environmental challenges and promote sustainable development.

Regional and global governance structures play a crucial role in shaping economic policies and addressing the challenges of Western hegemony. The reform of international financial institutions, such as the IMF and World Bank, has been a topic of discussion and debate, with calls for increased representation and voice for developing countries. Strengthening regional organizations and promoting South-South cooperation can also provide alternative pathways for economic development and reduce reliance on Western-dominated systems.

The future of global trade and economic policies will depend on the ability of nations and international institutions to navigate the complexities of an interconnected world. The pursuit of more equitable and sustainable economic practices requires a commitment to addressing the shortcomings of existing frameworks and exploring new approaches. By fostering international cooperation, promoting inclusive development, and addressing the challenges of Western hegemony, it is possible to work towards a global economic system that benefits all nations and peoples.

In conclusion, the impact of Western hegemony on global trade and economic policies is profound and multifaceted. While Western-dominated frameworks have facilitated economic growth and integration, they have also introduced significant challenges and inequalities. The influence of Western economic policies is evident across various sectors and regions, highlighting the need for reforms and alternative approaches to create a more equitable and sustainable global economic system. By addressing the shortcomings of existing frameworks and exploring new models, it is possible to work towards a global economy that benefits all nations and peoples.

Chapter 6: The Bretton Woods System and Economic Imperialism

The Bretton Woods system, established in the aftermath of World War II, was designed to create a framework for international economic cooperation. The system's architects—principally the United States and its allies—sought to rebuild war-torn economies and establish a stable global monetary order that would prevent the economic chaos that had preceded the war. What emerged from the Bretton Woods Conference in 1944 was a set of institutions, including the International Monetary Fund (IMF) and the World Bank, that would manage global financial interactions and promote economic stability. However, beneath the surface of these noble intentions lay an enduring system of economic imperialism, where the Western powers, particularly the United States, sought to entrench their dominance through economic means.

The Bretton Woods system was built on the premise that international trade and economic growth required stable currencies and cooperative international financial systems. The U.S. dollar, backed by gold, became the anchor of the new monetary order, with other currencies pegged to the dollar. This arrangement gave the United States unprecedented power in global financial affairs, as the dollar became the world's reserve currency. In theory, this was supposed to foster global stability, but in practice, it allowed the United States to wield disproportionate influence over the global economy.

The institutions created under the Bretton Woods system, namely the IMF and the World Bank, were established to provide financial assistance to countries in need and to promote development in impoverished regions. However, these institutions quickly became instruments of Western economic imperialism. The IMF, for example, often attached stringent conditions to its loans, requiring recipient countries to adopt policies of austerity, deregulation, and privatization—policies that frequently served Western corporate interests at the expense of local economies. Countries that failed to comply with IMF mandates often faced crippling debt burdens, leading to cycles of dependency on Western financial institutions.

One of the most significant impacts of the Bretton Woods system was the entrenchment of a global economic hierarchy, in which Western nations controlled the terms of trade, finance, and development. The World Bank, ostensibly created to support post-war reconstruction and development, also played a central role in this hierarchy. While the bank provided loans for infrastructure and development projects, these loans often came with conditions that aligned with the interests of Western corporations and governments. As a result, many developing nations found themselves indebted to the West, with their economies increasingly dependent on Western capital and expertise.

A key feature of the Bretton Woods system was the promotion of free trade and open markets. While this principle was intended to spur global economic growth, in practice, it disproportionately benefited Western countries, whose industries were already well-developed. Developing nations, on the other hand, struggled to compete in a global marketplace dominated by Western multinational corporations. Furthermore, the emphasis on free trade often undermined local industries in developing countries, as they were flooded with cheap imports from the West. This process of economic liberalization, which was championed by the IMF and the World Bank, frequently led to the deindustrialization of developing economies and the erosion of local livelihoods.

The Bretton Woods institutions also played a central role in shaping the economic policies of post-colonial states. In many cases, newly independent nations turned to the IMF and World Bank for financial assistance, only to find that the conditions attached to these loans undermined their sovereignty and economic independence. The structural adjustment programs (SAPs) promoted by these institutions in the 1980s and 1990s are a prime example of this. Under the guise of economic reform, the IMF and

World Bank imposed policies that prioritized debt repayment and fiscal discipline over social welfare and development. These programs often led to cuts in public services, such as healthcare and education, exacerbating poverty and inequality in the affected countries.

The experience of Latin America during the 1980s debt crisis illustrates the devastating impact of IMF and World Bank policies. Many countries in the region, burdened by debt accumulated during the 1970s, were forced to turn to the IMF for assistance. In exchange for loans, they were required to implement austerity measures, deregulate their economies, and open their markets to foreign investment. While these policies may have stabilized the financial situation in the short term, they also led to social unrest, rising unemployment, and deepening inequality. The "lost decade" of the 1980s in Latin America is a testament to the failure of the Bretton Woods institutions to promote genuine development.

In Africa, the legacy of the Bretton Woods system has been similarly damaging. Many African nations, seeking to build their economies after gaining independence, found themselves trapped in cycles of debt and dependency on Western financial institutions. The IMF and World Bank often imposed conditions that required African governments to prioritize debt repayment over social investment, leading to chronic underdevelopment and poverty. In many cases, the privatization and deregulation policies promoted by the IMF also opened the door for Western corporations to exploit Africa's natural resources, further entrenching economic imperialism.

While the Bretton Woods system officially ended in the early 1970s, when the United States abandoned the gold standard, the legacy of economic imperialism continues to shape the global economy. The IMF and World Bank remain powerful institutions, and their influence is still felt in developing nations around the world. The United States, which retains the largest voting share in both institutions, continues to use them as tools of economic diplomacy, leveraging financial aid and loans to advance its geopolitical interests.

In recent years, there has been growing criticism of the Bretton Woods institutions and their role in perpetuating global inequality.

Many argue that the IMF and World Bank have failed to adapt to the changing realities of the global economy, and that their policies continue to reflect the interests of Western powers at the expense of developing nations. Efforts to reform these institutions have been met with resistance, as the United States and other Western countries seek to maintain their dominance in global financial governance.

However, the rise of alternative financial institutions, such as China's Asian Infrastructure Investment Bank (AIIB) and the New Development Bank (NDB) created by the BRICS nations, suggests that the era of Western economic hegemony may be coming to an end. These institutions offer developing nations an alternative to the IMF and World Bank, and they have been particularly attractive to countries that are wary of the conditions attached to Western loans. While it remains to be seen whether these new institutions will offer a genuinely different model of development, their emergence reflects a growing desire among developing nations to challenge the economic imperialism of the Bretton Woods system.

In conclusion, the Bretton Woods system, while initially conceived as a means of promoting global economic stability, ultimately became a vehicle for Western economic imperialism. The institutions it created—the IMF and the World Bank—have played a central role in shaping the global economic order, often to the detriment of developing nations. Through policies of austerity, privatization, and deregulation, these institutions have entrenched a system of economic dependency that continues to exacerbate global inequality. While efforts to reform the Bretton Woods institutions have been slow and often ineffective, the rise of alternative financial institutions may offer hope for a more equitable global economic order in the future.

Chapter 7: Cultural Dominance and the Spread of Western Values

The influence of Western hegemony is not limited to economic and political spheres—it also extends deeply into the realm of culture. Through various mechanisms, including media, entertainment, education, and technology, Western values have been exported and entrenched across the globe. The process of cultural globalization, largely driven by Western powers, has had profound implications on local traditions, identities, and ways of life. While some argue that the spread of Western values has led to progress and modernization, others contend that it has eroded cultural diversity, reinforced neo-colonial power structures, and led to the imposition of foreign norms.

The roots of Western cultural dominance trace back to the colonial era, during which European powers imposed their languages, education systems, and belief systems on colonized regions. The legacy of colonialism established the foundation for Western cultural influence in many parts of the world. Over time, this influence has evolved into a more complex form of soft power, where Western values are transmitted not through direct coercion but through the allure and ubiquity of Western cultural products.

In the contemporary era, the role of mass media and entertainment in disseminating Western values cannot be overstated. Hollywood, for instance, is not just an entertainment powerhouse but also a vehicle for exporting American ideals. From movies and television shows to music and social media, Western cultural products often carry underlying messages about individualism, consumerism, freedom, and democracy. These products reach audiences worldwide, shaping perceptions, desires, and aspirations, particularly among younger generations. The portrayal of Western lifestyles in media often positions them as aspirational, contributing to the widespread acceptance of Western norms.

The global dominance of the English language is another key factor in the spread of Western values. As the lingua franca of international business, science, and diplomacy, English facilitates the transmission of Western ideas and knowledge. Educational institutions in many countries prioritize English-language learning, often at the expense of local languages and traditions. This phenomenon raises concerns about linguistic imperialism, as the growing emphasis on English can lead to the marginalization of indigenous languages and the erosion of cultural heritage.

Education systems around the world have also been shaped by Western values, particularly in former colonies. Western models of education often emphasize scientific rationalism, secularism, and individual achievement. While these principles have contributed to advancements in knowledge and human development, they have also clashed with local values and belief systems in some contexts. In regions where communal values, spiritual traditions, and collective well-being are central to social life, the imposition of Western education models can create cultural tensions and a sense of alienation.

Technology plays a critical role in the contemporary spread of Western values. The digital age has facilitated the rapid globalization of information, making it easier for Western cultural products to reach even the most remote parts of the world. Social media platforms like Facebook, Twitter, and Instagram—predominantly Western creations—serve as conduits for the dissemination of Western norms, from fashion and lifestyle trends to political ideologies. While these platforms provide opportunities for cross-cultural exchange, they can also contribute to the homogenization of global culture and the dominance of Western perspectives.

The spread of Western values through culture has been met with varying reactions across the world. In some cases, individuals and communities embrace elements of Western culture, seeing them as symbols of progress, modernity, and global connectedness. For instance, the adoption of Western technology, fashion, and entertainment can be viewed as a way to participate in a globalized world and access new opportunities. However, this embrace often comes with trade-offs, as individuals may feel pressure to conform to Western standards of success, beauty, and behavior, potentially leading to the erosion of local traditions and identities.

In contrast, other regions and communities resist the spread of Western values, viewing it as a form of cultural imperialism. This resistance is often rooted in a desire to preserve cultural heritage, religious beliefs, and social structures that are perceived to be under threat from Westernization. For example, in many parts of the Middle East and Africa, there are ongoing debates about the tension between traditional values and the influence of Western secularism and liberalism. In some cases, this tension has fueled nationalist or religious movements that seek to counter the encroachment of Western cultural norms.

The imposition of Western values is particularly evident in the realm of gender and family structures. Western ideas about gender equality, individual autonomy, and sexual freedom have had a profound impact on societies around the world, challenging traditional roles and norms. While these ideas have contributed to progress in areas such as women's rights and LGBTQ+ rights, they have also sparked cultural conflicts, particularly in conservative societies where traditional family structures and gender roles are deeply ingrained. In some contexts, the introduction of Western gender norms is seen as a threat to social cohesion and religious values.

The commercialization of culture is another consequence of Western cultural dominance. The global expansion of consumer capitalism, driven by Western multinational corporations, has commodified cultural products and practices. Traditional art forms, rituals, and symbols are often repackaged for global consumption, sometimes losing their original meaning in the process. This phenomenon, often referred to as "cultural appropriation," raises questions about the exploitation of indigenous cultures for profit, as well as the ethical implications of commodifying sacred or culturally significant practices.

Despite the challenges posed by Western cultural dominance,

there are also opportunities for cultural hybridity and exchange. In many cases, individuals and communities adapt and reinterpret Western values in ways that reflect their own cultural contexts. This process of cultural negotiation can lead to the creation of new, hybrid cultural forms that blend elements of Western and local traditions. For example, in the realm of music, genres like hip-hop and reggae have been embraced and adapted by artists around the world, who infuse these Western-originated styles with their own cultural influences and messages.

In addition, the rise of non-Western powers, such as China, India, and Brazil, has introduced new dynamics to the global cultural landscape. These emerging powers are increasingly exporting their own cultural products and values, challenging the dominance of Western cultural narratives. The growth of Bollywood, K-pop, and Chinese technology platforms like TikTok exemplifies the diversification of global cultural flows. This shift suggests that while Western hegemony remains influential, it is no longer unchallenged in the realm of culture.

The future of global culture will likely be shaped by a complex interplay between Western dominance, local resistance, and the rise of alternative cultural powers. As globalization continues to facilitate the exchange of ideas and values, there will be ongoing debates about the balance between preserving cultural diversity and participating in a shared global culture. The challenge for policymakers, cultural leaders, and communities will be to find ways to navigate these tensions in ways that respect cultural pluralism while fostering global cooperation and understanding.

In conclusion, Western cultural dominance has had a profound impact on global societies, shaping everything from media and entertainment to education and gender norms. While the spread of Western values has brought about significant changes and challenges, it has also sparked resistance and efforts to preserve local traditions. The ongoing process of cultural globalization will continue to evolve, influenced by both the enduring power of Western hegemony and the emergence of new cultural forces. As societies around the world grapple with the consequences of cultural exchange, the importance of fostering respect for cultural diversity and promoting equitable cultural relations remains paramount.

Broken Promises: Western Hegemony and Global Turmoil

Broken Promises: Western Hegemony and Global Turmoil

Chapter 8: The Neoliberal Era and the Global South

The rise of neoliberalism in the late 20th century marked a profound shift in global economic policy, fundamentally altering the relationship between the Global North and the Global South. Neoliberalism, with its emphasis on free markets, deregulation, privatization, and minimal state intervention, was presented as the path to prosperity for all nations. Its proponents argued that by opening up their economies to international trade and investment, countries in the Global South could benefit from the same kind of rapid economic growth that had propelled Western nations to global dominance. However, for many in the Global South, the reality of the neoliberal era has been far more complex and, in many cases, detrimental.

The neoliberal era began in earnest in the 1970s and 1980s, driven by the economic policies of leaders like Margaret Thatcher in the United Kingdom and Ronald Reagan in the United States. These policies were quickly adopted by international institutions such as the International Monetary Fund (IMF) and the World Bank, which began conditioning their loans to developing nations on the implementation of neoliberal reforms. These reforms, known as Structural Adjustment Programs (SAPs), required countries in the Global South to reduce public spending, deregulate their economies, and privatize state-owned enterprises. While these measures were intended to stimulate economic growth and attract foreign investment, they often had devastating social and economic consequences for the populations of these countries.

One of the most significant impacts of neoliberal policies in the Global South was the dismantling of social safety nets and public services. In countries across Africa, Latin America, and Asia, governments were forced to cut spending on education, healthcare, and welfare in order to meet the fiscal targets set by the IMF and World Bank. As a result, millions of people were left without access to basic services, exacerbating poverty and inequality. In many cases, the privatization of essential services such as water, electricity, and healthcare led to price increases that put these services out of reach for the poorest segments of society.

The emphasis on deregulation and free trade also had far-reaching consequences for the economies of the Global South. While neoliberal theorists argued that opening up markets would create new opportunities for economic growth, in practice, it often left developing nations at the mercy of global market forces beyond their control. Many countries in the Global South, particularly in Africa and Latin America, were encouraged to shift their economies towards the production of export commodities such as oil, minerals, and cash crops. This made them highly vulnerable to fluctuations in global commodity prices, as well as to the exploitative practices of multinational corporations.

In addition to these economic vulnerabilities, neoliberal policies often exacerbated social tensions in the Global South. The emphasis on individualism, competition, and the reduction of state intervention undermined traditional social structures and communal forms of support, particularly in rural areas. In many countries, the shift towards neoliberalism was accompanied by an increase in inequality, as the benefits of economic liberalization were concentrated in the hands of a small elite, while the majority of the population saw little improvement in their living standards.

One of the most striking examples of the impact of neoliberalism on the Global South is found in Latin America, where countries such as Mexico, Brazil, and Argentina implemented sweeping neoliberal reforms during the 1980s and 1990s. In Mexico, the signing of the North American Free Trade Agreement (NAFTA) in 1994 was hailed as a triumph of neoliberalism, promising to bring economic growth and prosperity by integrating the Mexican economy with those of the United States and Canada. However, while NAFTA did lead to increased trade and investment, it also had devastating consequences for many Mexican workers and farmers. Small-scale farmers, in particular, were unable to compete with heavily subsidized agricultural imports from the United States, leading to widespread rural poverty and forcing many to migrate to urban areas or cross the border into the U.S. in search of work.

The neoliberal era also saw a dramatic increase in the power and influence of multinational corporations, which played a central role in shaping the economic policies of countries in the Global South. These corporations, often based in the Global North, were able to exploit the weak regulatory frameworks and cheap labor available in many developing nations, extracting enormous profits while contributing little to the local economies. In some cases, multinational corporations were able to exert more influence over the economic policies of developing nations than the governments themselves, leading to a form of economic imperialism that closely resembled the colonial era.

The rise of neoliberalism also had significant political consequences in the Global South. The implementation of neoliberal policies often required the suppression of labor unions, social movements, and other forms of political opposition. In some cases, governments resorted to authoritarian measures to push through unpopular neoliberal reforms, leading to increased political repression and human rights abuses. In countries such as Chile, Argentina, and Brazil, military dictatorships played a key role in implementing neoliberal policies, often with the support of Western powers.

Despite the promises of neoliberalism, the economic outcomes for many countries in the Global South were far from positive. While some countries, such as China and India, were able to achieve rapid economic growth by embracing aspects of neoliberalism, many others saw little improvement in their living standards. In sub-Saharan Africa, for example, neoliberal policies failed to deliver the kind of sustained economic growth that had been promised, and many countries remained trapped in cycles of debt and poverty.

The legacy of the neoliberal era in the Global South is one of deepening inequality, social unrest, and economic dependency. While neoliberalism was supposed to create a level playing field in the global economy, it often reinforced existing power imbalances between the Global North and the Global South. The economic policies of the IMF, World Bank, and other international institutions were frequently designed to serve the interests of Western powers and multinational corporations, rather than the needs of the populations of developing nations.

In recent years, there has been growing resistance to neoliberalism in the Global South, as social movements, labor unions, and progressive political parties have challenged the dominance of free market ideology. In Latin America, the so-called "Pink Tide" of left-wing governments in the 2000s, led by figures such as Hugo Chávez in Venezuela and Evo Morales in Bolivia, sought to reverse the neoliberal policies of their predecessors and implement alternative models of development based on social justice and economic sovereignty. These movements have faced significant challenges, both from domestic elites and from Western powers that continue to promote neoliberalism as the only viable path to development.

Despite these challenges, the rise of new economic powers such as China and the increasing influence of alternative global institutions such as the BRICS group suggest that the neoliberal era may be coming to an end. As countries in the Global South seek to assert their independence and chart their own paths to development, the future of the global economic order remains uncertain. However, what is clear is that the neoliberal model, which has dominated global economic policy for the past several decades, has failed to deliver on its promises for much of the world.

In conclusion, the neoliberal era has been marked by profound economic and social upheaval in the Global South. While its proponents claimed that free markets, deregulation, and privatization would lead to prosperity for all, the reality has been far more complex and, in many cases, damaging. For many countries in the Global South, neoliberal policies have led to increased inequality, poverty, and economic dependency on the Global North. As the world moves towards a new economic order, it is essential that the lessons of the neoliberal era are learned, and that future models of development prioritize the needs and aspirations of the people of the Global South, rather than the interests of multinational corporations and Western powers.

Chapter 9: The Environmental Consequences of Western Development

For centuries, Western development has been synonymous with economic expansion, technological innovation, and industrial progress. This model of growth, driven by capitalism and consumerism, has shaped the global economy and set the blueprint for development around the world. However, this relentless pursuit of progress has come at a tremendous cost to the environment. Western development has not only depleted natural resources but also contributed to widespread environmental degradation, from deforestation and pollution to the catastrophic impacts of climate change.

The roots of this environmental destruction can be traced back to the Industrial Revolution in the 18th and 19th centuries, a period of intense industrialization that fundamentally altered the relationship between humans and nature. The rise of factories, mass production, and mechanized agriculture required vast amounts of raw materials, leading to the exploitation of natural resources on an unprecedented scale. Forests were cleared for timber and farmland, rivers were dammed for energy, and fossil fuels—coal, oil, and natural gas—became the lifeblood of Western economies. This insatiable demand for resources set the stage for the environmental crises we face today.

One of the most visible environmental impacts of Western development is the depletion of natural resources. For centuries, Western powers have extracted vast quantities of raw materials from the earth, often without regard for the long-term consequences.

The logging industry, for example, has been responsible for the destruction of large swathes of the world's forests, particularly in North America, Europe, and later, tropical regions like the Amazon rainforest. Deforestation not only destroys ecosystems and displaces wildlife, but it also contributes to climate change by reducing the earth's ability to absorb carbon dioxide from the atmosphere.

In addition to deforestation, Western development has also led to the overexploitation of other natural resources, such as water, minerals, and fossil fuels. In many cases, the extraction of these resources has been carried out in a manner that prioritizes short-term profits over long-term sustainability. For example, the oil industry, which has been at the heart of Western economic development since the early 20th century, has been responsible for some of the most significant environmental disasters in history, from oil spills to the contamination of water sources and ecosystems.

The extraction of natural resources is not only destructive in itself, but it also leads to pollution, one of the most pervasive environmental consequences of Western development. The burning of fossil fuels for energy and transportation is a major source of air pollution, releasing harmful gases such as carbon dioxide (CO_2), sulfur dioxide (SO_2), and nitrogen oxides (NO_x) into the atmosphere. These emissions contribute to the formation of smog, acid rain, and respiratory illnesses in humans, as well as the destruction of ecosystems.

Water pollution is another critical issue linked to Western development. Industrial activities, particularly mining, manufacturing, and agriculture, generate large amounts of toxic waste, which often ends up in rivers, lakes, and oceans. In many cases, these pollutants, which include heavy metals, chemicals, and plastics, have devastating effects on aquatic life and human health. The oceans, in particular, have become a dumping ground for plastic waste, with millions of tons of plastic entering the marine environment each year. This plastic pollution has far-reaching consequences, from the poisoning of marine species to the contamination of the food chain.

Perhaps the most far-reaching environmental consequence of Western development is climate change, a global crisis that threatens the very survival of life on earth. Climate change is primarily driven by the burning of fossil fuels, which releases greenhouse gases (GHGs) such as CO_2 and methane into the atmosphere. These gases trap heat, causing the earth's temperature to rise—a phenomenon known as global warming. The rise in global temperatures has led to a host of environmental impacts, including melting glaciers, rising sea levels, more frequent and severe weather events, and shifts in ecosystems and biodiversity.

The Western model of development has been particularly damaging in its reliance on fossil fuels as the primary source of energy. For more than a century, coal, oil, and natural gas have powered the economic growth of the West, fueling everything from factories and transportation to electricity generation and home heating. However, the environmental costs of this reliance on fossil fuels have been staggering. The combustion of coal and oil, in particular, has been responsible for much of the world's CO_2 emissions, which have increased dramatically since the Industrial Revolution. Today, the United States and the European Union are among the largest historical emitters of greenhouse gases, and their legacy of emissions continues to drive climate change.

The effects of climate change are already being felt around the world, but they are particularly severe in vulnerable regions such as the Global South, where many countries are ill-equipped to deal with the consequences. Rising sea levels, for example, threaten to submerge low-lying island nations and coastal cities, while more frequent and intense storms, droughts, and heatwaves are exacerbating food and water insecurity in many developing countries. Ironically, these countries, which have contributed the least to global emissions, are often the most affected by climate change, highlighting the deep environmental injustices that have emerged from Western development.

In addition to climate change, Western development has also contributed to the loss of biodiversity, a crisis that is often referred to as the "sixth mass extinction." The destruction of habitats through deforestation, urbanization, and industrial agriculture has led to the extinction of countless species, from large mammals like tigers and elephants to smaller creatures like insects and amphibians. The loss of biodiversity has far-reaching consequences for ecosystems, which rely on a delicate balance of species to function properly. The decline of pollinators like bees, for example, threatens global food production, while the loss of keystone species like wolves can lead to the collapse of entire ecosystems.

One of the key drivers of biodiversity loss is industrial agriculture, which has been promoted as a solution to feeding the world's growing population. However, the Western model of industrial farming, with its reliance on monoculture, chemical fertilizers, and pesticides, has been devastating for the environment. Monoculture farming, in particular, depletes soil nutrients and reduces biodiversity, while the overuse of pesticides and fertilizers pollutes water sources and harms wildlife. In many cases, industrial agriculture has displaced traditional, sustainable farming practices, particularly in the Global South, leading to further environmental degradation and food insecurity.

The environmental consequences of Western development are not confined to the natural world; they also have profound social and economic implications. Environmental degradation often disproportionately affects marginalized communities, particularly in the Global South, where poverty, lack of infrastructure, and political instability exacerbate the impacts of climate change and pollution. In many cases, these communities are forced to bear the brunt of environmental destruction caused by Western corporations and governments, despite having contributed little to the problem. This has led to growing calls for environmental justice, a movement that seeks to address the inequalities that arise from the intersection of environmental and social issues.

One of the most striking examples of environmental injustice can be seen in the case of multinational corporations operating in the Global South. These corporations, often based in Western countries, frequently exploit the natural resources of developing nations, leaving behind environmental devastation and social unrest. In many cases, local communities are left to deal with the consequences, whether it be polluted water sources, deforestation, or the loss of livelihoods. This pattern of exploitation mirrors the colonial era, where Western powers extracted resources from their colonies without regard for the long-term consequences.

The case of oil extraction in Nigeria's Niger Delta is a stark example of the environmental and social consequences of Western development. For decades, multinational oil companies, including Shell and Chevron, have extracted billions of dollars' worth of oil from the region, while local communities have suffered from widespread pollution and environmental degradation. Oil spills, gas flaring, and the destruction of wetlands have devastated the region's ecosystems, while local fishermen and farmers have seen their livelihoods disappear. Despite the wealth generated by oil extraction, the Niger Delta remains one of the poorest regions in Nigeria, highlighting the stark disconnect between Western development and the well-being of local communities.

As the environmental consequences of Western development become increasingly apparent, there is a growing recognition that the current model of economic growth is unsustainable. The depletion of natural resources, the destruction of ecosystems, and the threat of climate change all point to the need for a new approach to development—one that prioritizes environmental sustainability and social justice over short-term economic gains. This has led to the rise of movements such as degrowth, which advocate for a radical rethinking of economic systems and a shift towards more sustainable, equitable forms of development.

The dominance of Western ideologies in development has often promoted growth at the expense of environmental well-being, prioritizing industrial output and consumption. One of the enduring legacies of this has been the destruction of ecosystems worldwide. When one examines the consequences of Western agricultural practices, particularly the Green Revolution of the mid-20th century, it becomes clear that while increasing food production, it also introduced harmful environmental effects that continue to reverberate globally.

The Green Revolution, which promised to alleviate hunger through the introduction of high-yielding crop varieties, chemical fertilizers, and pesticides, had unintended environmental costs. It degraded soils, depleted water resources, and contributed to the loss of biodiversity as monoculture replaced diverse agricultural practices. As these technologies were exported to developing nations, particularly in Asia and Latin America, countries were encouraged to adopt practices that prioritized short-term agricultural output over sustainable land management. In the process, traditional farming knowledge, often in harmony with the environment, was marginalized in favor of an industrial model that required intensive chemical inputs and irrigation. These choices, guided by Western agricultural practices, continue to strain ecosystems globally.

The consequences of Western industrial expansion have also led to the global spread of toxic waste. E-waste, or electronic waste, is one glaring example of how the cycle of Western consumerism has burdened the environment. As the demand for electronics—driven by technological advancements and capitalist markets—skyrocketed in the West, developing countries became the dumping ground for obsolete or discarded electronics. Countries in Africa and Asia, such as Ghana and India, have become notorious for their electronic waste dumps. Here, Western e-waste is dismantled in unsafe conditions, poisoning local environments and causing significant health problems for workers exposed to harmful materials like lead, mercury, and cadmium.

The externalization of waste is not just limited to electronic products. Western nations have long practiced a system where they export environmental degradation to poorer nations. Toxic chemicals, outdated pesticides, and hazardous materials banned or regulated in Western countries are often sold to or dumped in countries in the Global South, where regulations are less stringent or nonexistent. This practice ensures that the environmental costs of consumption in the West are borne by some of the world's most vulnerable communities, entrenching patterns of environmental injustice. The global shipping of waste products from the West to other countries serves as a stark reminder of how environmental degradation is outsourced to preserve the illusion of sustainable consumption in wealthier nations.

Perhaps one of the most significant environmental injustices has been the effects of climate change on indigenous populations. Indigenous peoples, often living in close connection with their environment, have been disproportionately affected by the environmental changes brought on by Western development. The destruction of rainforests in Brazil, driven by agricultural expansion for beef and soy exports primarily destined for Western markets, has encroached on indigenous territories, disrupting their way of life and destroying the ecosystems they depend upon. Similarly, in North

America and Australia, indigenous communities have been marginalized as industrial expansion—driven by mining, logging, and infrastructure projects—has systematically eroded their land rights and access to resources.

The extractive industries, particularly mining, are a key example of how Western development has led to environmental destruction on a massive scale. The demand for minerals and metals in Western economies has driven mining operations deep into fragile ecosystems. The consequences of mining are often devastating: deforestation, loss of biodiversity, water contamination, and soil degradation. The expansion of mining in countries like the Democratic Republic of Congo and Peru has had profound environmental impacts. Western companies, in their quest for precious metals such as cobalt, used in the production of electronics and electric vehicles, have contributed to deforestation, pollution, and the destruction of local environments. Despite claims of corporate social responsibility, the environmental degradation caused by these industries continues to expand, leaving lasting scars on the earth and contributing to global inequality.

One particularly stark environmental issue tied to Western development is the fossil fuel industry. Western energy companies, through their global reach and influence, have entrenched reliance on oil and gas, not only within their own economies but also in developing nations. These companies have contributed directly to environmental degradation through oil spills, gas flaring, and the destruction of ecosystems, particularly in oil-rich regions like Nigeria and Venezuela. The environmental damage wrought by fossil fuel extraction and consumption is most clearly visible in events like the 2010 Deepwater Horizon oil spill in the Gulf of Mexico, which caused massive ecological destruction. But these incidents are not isolated to the West—communities around the world, particularly in the Global South, continue to bear the brunt of these environmental disasters, often without the capacity or infrastructure to manage the fallout.

In the Arctic, climate change is having profound effects on the fragile ecosystems. As global temperatures rise, the Arctic ice sheets are melting at alarming rates, opening up new areas for oil exploration and shipping routes. Western governments and corporations, rather than addressing the root causes of climate change, have viewed the melting Arctic as a new frontier for economic exploitation. Oil companies from Western nations, such as ExxonMobil and Shell, have invested in Arctic oil exploration, further exacerbating the environmental destruction of one of the world's most sensitive ecosystems. The irony of this approach—profiting from the very crisis they have helped create—is emblematic of the Western model of development.

As the world grapples with the environmental consequences of this development model, the issue of environmental refugees is becoming increasingly urgent. People displaced by environmental disasters, many of which have been exacerbated by Western-driven climate change, face an uncertain future. Rising sea levels, extreme weather events, and desertification are displacing millions of people, particularly in regions such as the Pacific Islands, sub-Saharan Africa, and South Asia. These environmental refugees, many of whom come from developing nations, are often forced to migrate to cities or other countries, where they face precarious living conditions and, in some cases, hostile political climates. Western nations, while historically responsible for much of the carbon emissions driving climate change, have largely failed to offer adequate support or refuge for these displaced populations, further deepening the divide between the Global North and South.

The environmental toll of Western development is not merely an unintended consequence of economic growth but an intrinsic part of a system that prioritizes profit and consumption over sustainability and the well-being of future generations. The deepening climate crisis, loss of biodiversity, and environmental degradation all point to the urgent need for a fundamental rethink of the Western model of development. Yet, despite the growing awareness of these issues, political and economic systems remain resistant to the transformative changes necessary to avert ecological disaster.

If there is a glimmer of hope, it lies in the growing environmental movements challenging the status quo. Across the world, activists, scientists, and communities are advocating for alternative models of development that prioritize environmental sustainability, social justice, and the rights of future generations. Movements like Extinction Rebellion and Fridays for Future have raised awareness about the environmental destruction caused by Western development and have called for immediate action to combat climate change and biodiversity loss. Indigenous movements, in particular, have played a crucial role in advocating for the protection of natural ecosystems and the recognition of indigenous land rights, challenging the Western paradigm of development that has long marginalized their voices.

The environmental consequences of Western development are a testament to the profound disconnect between humanity and the natural world that has been exacerbated by industrialization, capitalism, and consumerism. The question facing the world today is whether we can move beyond this destructive model of development and create a future that is environmentally sustainable, just, and equitable. The answer will require not only a rethinking of economic and political systems but also a profound shift in values, away from the pursuit of endless growth and toward a more harmonious relationship with the planet.

The path forward will not be easy, but as the environmental crises deepen, it is becoming increasingly clear that the Western model of development is unsustainable. The choice is stark: continue down the current path of environmental destruction or embrace a new vision of development that prioritizes the well-being of the planet and all its inhabitants. The future of humanity—and the planet—depends on the choices we make today.

Chapter 10: The Rise of New Powers and the Challenge to Western Hegemony

The 21st century marks a period of profound global change in which the unipolar world order, dominated by Western powers—particularly the United States—has begun to face significant challenges. This chapter explores the rise of new global powers, such as China, Russia, India, and others, which are reshaping the geopolitical landscape, contesting Western hegemony, and advocating for a multipolar world. The rise of these nations is not just a geopolitical shift; it represents a challenge to Western-dominated institutions, values, and models of governance. The question of whether these new powers can upend Western dominance or merely alter the existing order is central to understanding contemporary global politics.

For much of the 20th century, the United States and its Western allies established and maintained an international order that was predicated on economic liberalization, democracy, and security cooperation. The Bretton Woods institutions, NATO, and the United Nations were tools to solidify Western control, with the United States at the helm of the global system. However, as new powers have emerged and gained influence, they have increasingly sought to redefine the norms, institutions, and frameworks that govern international relations. In particular, the rapid rise of China, the resurgence of Russia, and the growing influence of middle powers like India and Brazil have challenged Western dominance.

China's rise is arguably the most significant development in global politics since the end of the Cold War. The country's astonishing economic growth over the past few decades has transformed it into a global superpower. China's political leaders have been strategic in using economic might to bolster their influence across the world, particularly in Asia, Africa, and Latin America. Through initiatives such as the Belt and Road Initiative (BRI), China has cultivated relationships with a wide array of developing countries, offering them alternatives to Western financial institutions like the World Bank and the International Monetary Fund (IMF). By providing infrastructure investment, loans, and trade opportunities, China has garnered influence and loyalty, positioning itself as a champion of the developing world and a counterbalance to Western power.

Chinese foreign policy, especially under Xi Jinping, represents a significant departure from previous decades, when China maintained a relatively low profile in international politics. Today, China is assertively expanding its military and economic influence in the Indo-Pacific region, engaging in diplomatic efforts to reshape global governance, and promoting its model of authoritarian capitalism as an alternative to Western democracy. This growing assertiveness has led to increased tension with the United States and its allies, with some analysts even warning of a new Cold War between China and the West.

One of the most visible signs of China's challenge to Western hegemony is its increasing influence in international organizations. China has become a major player in the United Nations, the World Health Organization, and other global bodies, often using its influence to promote its interests and protect its allies, such as North Korea and Myanmar, from international scrutiny. By gaining leadership roles in these institutions, China has also begun to reshape global governance in a way that reflects its own interests, often at the expense of Western powers. For example, China has advocated for a more state-centric approach to development and governance, in contrast to the Western emphasis on human rights and liberal democracy.

Russia, too, has re-emerged as a significant power in the global arena, particularly in the context of its foreign policy under Vladimir Putin. Since the early 2000s, Russia has sought to reassert itself as a great power, challenging Western influence in Eastern Europe, the Middle East, and beyond. The annexation of Crimea in 2014, military interventions in Syria, and alleged interference in Western elections are all part of Russia's broader strategy to undermine the Western-dominated global order and assert its own influence.

Russia's strategy has been multifaceted. It has sought to weaken NATO by exploiting divisions within the alliance, particularly by courting countries with authoritarian leaders or those that are critical of the European Union. In addition, Russia has used energy as a tool of influence, particularly in Europe, where many countries depend on Russian oil and gas. This energy dependence has given Russia leverage over the EU, complicating efforts to impose sanctions or respond to Russian aggression. Moreover, Russia has cultivated relationships with countries that are either adversarial to or skeptical of Western influence, such as Iran, Turkey, and China, forming alliances that challenge Western norms and policies.

Russia's actions have provoked strong reactions from the West, leading to sanctions, diplomatic isolation, and a renewed emphasis on NATO's role in deterring Russian aggression. However, these measures have not deterred Russia from pursuing its geopolitical goals, and in some cases, they have driven Russia closer to China, creating a potential counterbalance to Western power. The deepening cooperation between Russia and China, especially in areas such as energy and military technology, has raised concerns in the West about the emergence of a new authoritarian bloc that could challenge the liberal international order.

India, while often positioned as a democratic counterbalance to China in Asia, has also pursued a more independent foreign policy that does not always align with Western interests. Under Prime Minister Narendra Modi, India has sought to enhance its regional and global influence by building stronger relationships with a wide array of countries, including Russia, Japan, and the United States. India's foreign policy is driven by a desire to maintain strategic autonomy and avoid becoming overly reliant on any one power, particularly as tensions with China have increased.

India's growing economic and military power has made it a key player in global geopolitics. The country's focus on technological innovation, defense modernization, and economic growth has allowed it to carve out a unique position in the global order. India's membership in multilateral organizations, such as the BRICS (Brazil,

Russia, India, China, and South Africa), the Shanghai Cooperation Organization (SCO), and its involvement in regional forums like the South Asian Association for Regional Cooperation (SAARC), highlight its ambition to play a leadership role in shaping the future of global governance.

However, India's rise has also exposed the limitations of Western attempts to maintain hegemony. While India shares many values with Western democracies, such as a commitment to democratic governance, it has not fully aligned itself with Western strategic objectives. For example, India has maintained a neutral stance on many global issues, including relations with Iran and Russia, and has resisted calls from the United States to take a more confrontational approach toward China. This has led to a more complex and nuanced geopolitical environment, where emerging powers like India pursue their own interests without necessarily aligning with or opposing the West.

Brazil, though often overlooked in discussions of global power, has also played a critical role in challenging Western hegemony. As the largest country in Latin America, Brazil has positioned itself as a leader in the Global South, advocating for greater representation of developing countries in global institutions. Brazil has been a vocal critic of Western dominance in institutions such as the IMF and the World Trade Organization (WTO), arguing that these institutions are biased in favor of wealthy countries and do not adequately address the needs of the developing world.

Under leaders like Luiz Inácio Lula da Silva, Brazil has pursued an independent foreign policy, strengthening ties with other emerging powers in the BRICS grouping and advocating for reforms to global governance that reflect the changing balance of power. Brazil has also played a key role in regional organizations such as Mercosur, promoting economic integration and cooperation among Latin American countries. However, Brazil's global influence has been hampered by domestic political challenges, including corruption scandals, economic crises, and political polarization. These challenges have limited Brazil's ability to fully capitalize on its potential as a global power, but the country remains an important player in the broader contest between the West and the rest of the world.

As these new powers rise, they are not simply challenging Western hegemony by building their own economic and military capabilities. They are also challenging the ideological foundations of the Western-led global order. The spread of authoritarian capitalism, championed by countries like China and Russia, offers an alternative model of governance that contrasts sharply with Western democracy. In this model, economic growth and political stability are prioritized over individual freedoms and human rights. This model has proven attractive to many developing countries, particularly those with weak institutions or authoritarian leaders, who see it as a path to modernization without the disruptions that often accompany liberal democracy.

The challenge posed by new powers is not limited to geopolitics and governance models. It extends to the realm of global economics. The rise of new economic powers has led to the creation of alternative financial institutions, such as the Asian Infrastructure Investment Bank (AIIB), which are designed to challenge the dominance of Western-led institutions like the World Bank and the IMF. These new institutions offer developing countries alternative sources of funding for infrastructure and development projects, often with fewer political and economic conditions attached than those imposed by Western institutions.

This shift in global economics is also reflected in the growing importance of regional trade agreements that bypass Western-dominated trade forums. The Regional Comprehensive Economic Partnership (RCEP), which includes China, India, Japan, and other Asia-Pacific countries, is one such example. This mega trade deal represents a significant realignment of global trade, with implications for the West's ability to shape the rules and norms of global commerce.

The rise of new powers and their challenge to Western hegemony also has significant implications for global security. As new powers assert themselves on the global stage, they have increasingly sought to develop military capabilities that rival those of the West. China's military modernization, for example, has been a central component of its strategy to challenge Western dominance, particularly in the Asia-Pacific region. China's growing naval power, advancements in missile technology, and investments in cybersecurity have alarmed the United States and its allies, leading to a series of military confrontations and diplomatic standoffs in the South China Sea, Taiwan Strait, and other strategic areas. China's militarization of disputed territories in the South China Sea, along with its aggressive rhetoric regarding Taiwan, has underscored its intention to assert control over its perceived sphere of influence, directly challenging U.S. military presence in the region.

Similarly, Russia's military actions, particularly its annexation of Crimea and involvement in conflicts in Syria and Ukraine, have showcased its willingness to use military force to achieve geopolitical objectives. Russia's tactics, which often combine conventional military operations with cyber warfare and disinformation campaigns, represent a new type of hybrid warfare that has challenged Western security paradigms. These actions have not only destabilized regions but have also put pressure on Western military alliances, particularly NATO, to rethink their strategic responses to a more assertive Russia.

In the context of global security, one of the most significant developments in recent years has been the increasing collaboration between China and Russia. While their relationship has often been characterized by mutual suspicion, particularly during the Cold War, recent years have seen the two countries draw closer together as they confront common adversaries in the West. This collaboration has taken the form of joint military exercises, increased trade and energy partnerships, and diplomatic coordination on key global issues, such as opposing Western intervention in Syria and Venezuela. The deepening Sino-Russian relationship represents a formidable challenge to the Western-dominated global order, as it combines the economic and technological power of China with the military and energy resources of Russia.

India, while not directly aligned with China and Russia, has also been expanding its military capabilities in response to perceived threats from both China and Pakistan. India's development of nuclear weapons, coupled with its increasing defense cooperation with countries like the United States, Japan, and Australia, has made it a key player in the Indo-Pacific region. The formation of the Quadrilateral Security Dialogue (Quad), an informal security arrangement between the United States, Japan, India, and Australia, is one of the most visible signs of a new security architecture emerging in the region, aimed at countering China's growing influence.

The rise of new powers and their challenge to Western hegemony has also sparked a broader ideological conflict. The post-World War II international order was built on the principles of liberal democracy, free markets, and human rights, ideals that were championed by the West and institutionalized in global governance structures. However, the rise of authoritarian powers like China and Russia has presented an alternative model of governance that prioritizes state control, economic growth, and stability over individual freedoms and democratic accountability.

China's model of authoritarian capitalism, in particular, has gained traction in many parts of the world. By combining state control with market reforms, China has achieved rapid economic growth without the political liberalization that Western theorists once assumed was necessary for development. This success has led many developing countries to look to China as a model, particularly those with authoritarian leaders who are wary of Western demands for political reform. China's ability to provide economic assistance without the political strings attached—such as demands for democratization or human rights improvements—has made it an attractive partner for many countries in Africa, Latin America, and Southeast Asia.

Russia, too, has promoted an alternative model of governance that emphasizes strong state control and opposition to Western liberalism. Under Vladimir Putin, Russia has positioned itself as a defender of traditional values and national sovereignty, often in direct opposition to what it perceives as Western moral and political decay. This narrative has resonated with populist movements in Europe and the United States, which have become increasingly disillusioned with liberal democracy and globalism.

The ideological challenge posed by these new powers is not limited to their own borders. Through a combination of state-controlled media, cyber operations, and diplomatic initiatives, both China and Russia have sought to influence political outcomes in the West. Russia's alleged interference in the 2016 U.S. presidential election, as well as its support for far-right and populist movements in Europe, has been part of a broader strategy to weaken Western unity and undermine democratic institutions. China's influence campaigns, which have targeted media, academia, and political institutions in the West, aim to promote a more favorable image of China and suppress criticism of its human rights record, particularly regarding its actions in Hong Kong and Xinjiang.

The challenge to Western hegemony also extends to the economic realm, where the rise of new powers has led to a reevaluation of global trade, finance, and investment. China's Belt and Road Initiative (BRI), a massive infrastructure and investment project that spans Asia, Africa, and Europe, is perhaps the most ambitious example of how new powers are reshaping the global economic landscape. Through the BRI, China has invested billions of dollars in infrastructure projects, creating new trade routes and economic ties that bypass traditional Western-dominated financial institutions.

Critics of the BRI have argued that it represents a form of "debt-trap diplomacy," where developing countries become financially dependent on China and lose control over their own resources and infrastructure. Proponents, however, argue that the BRI provides much-needed investment in regions that have been neglected by Western powers and that it offers a new model of South-South cooperation. Regardless of the criticisms, there is no doubt that the BRI has shifted the balance of global economic power, challenging the dominance of Western financial institutions like the World Bank and the IMF.

Russia, too, has sought to challenge Western economic dominance, particularly through its role as a major energy supplier. Russia's vast reserves of oil and natural gas have given it significant leverage over countries that depend on its energy exports, particularly in Europe. The Nord Stream 2 pipeline, which transports Russian gas directly to Germany, bypassing Ukraine, has been a particularly contentious project, with critics arguing that it increases Europe's dependence on Russian energy and undermines Western efforts to isolate Russia politically. By using energy as a geopolitical tool, Russia has been able to exert influence over countries that might otherwise be aligned with the West.

India, while not directly challenging Western economic institutions, has also pursued a more independent economic policy that reflects its desire to be a global power in its own right. India's decision to withdraw from the Regional Comprehensive Economic Partnership (RCEP), despite being a key player in its negotiations, is indicative of its desire to protect its own economic interests and maintain strategic autonomy. India has also been a vocal advocate for reforming global financial institutions to better reflect the realities of a multipolar world, where emerging powers like India and Brazil have a greater say in global economic governance.

The rise of new powers and the challenge to Western hegemony has also had significant implications for the global environment. As countries like China and India have industrialized, they have become major contributors to global greenhouse gas emissions, leading to growing concerns about climate change. The West, which has historically been the largest contributor to global emissions, has been slow to address these concerns, and new powers have often resisted Western calls for stricter environmental regulations, arguing that they should not be punished for the environmental damage caused by Western industrialization.

China, in particular, has been at the center of the global debate on climate change. As the world's largest emitter of carbon dioxide, China has faced growing pressure to reduce its emissions and transition to a more sustainable energy system. While China has made significant investments in renewable energy and has committed to becoming carbon neutral by 2060, its continued reliance on coal and other fossil fuels has raised questions about its commitment to global climate goals. Moreover, China's Belt and Road Initiative has often involved the construction of coal-fired power plants in developing countries, further contributing to global emissions.

India, too, faces significant challenges in balancing its economic development with environmental sustainability. With a population of over 1.3 billion people and a rapidly growing economy, India's energy demands are expected to increase significantly in the coming decades. While India has made strides in renewable energy, particularly in solar power, it continues to rely heavily on coal and other fossil fuels to meet its energy needs. This reliance has made it difficult for India to commit to the same level of emissions reductions as Western countries, which have already reaped the benefits of industrialization.

The rise of new powers and the challenge to Western hegemony also raise broader questions about the future of global governance. As new powers assert themselves on the global stage, they have increasingly sought to reshape the institutions that govern international relations. China and Russia, in particular, have been critical of Western-dominated institutions like the United Nations, the World Bank, and the IMF, arguing that they are biased in favor of Western interests and do not adequately represent the needs of developing countries.

In response, new powers have sought to create alternative institutions that reflect their own interests and values. The Shanghai Cooperation Organization (SCO), the BRICS grouping, and the Asian Infrastructure Investment Bank (AIIB) are all examples of how new powers are building parallel institutions that challenge the dominance of Western-led organizations. These institutions have provided a platform for new powers to coordinate their efforts, share resources, and promote their own models of governance and development.

The rise of new powers and their challenge to Western hegemony represent one of the most significant shifts in global politics in recent history. As these powers continue to assert themselves on the global stage, they are reshaping the norms, institutions, and frameworks that govern international relations. Whether this leads to the emergence of a truly multipolar world or simply a reconfiguration of the existing order remains to be seen. What is clear, however, is that the era of uncontested Western dominance is coming to an end, and the future of global governance will be shaped by a more diverse array of actors, interests, and ideologies.

Broken Promises: Western Hegemony and Global Turmoil

Chapter 11: Broken Promises and the Future of Global Governance

In the latter half of the 20th century, the Western world stood at the helm of a global order that had promised peace, development, and cooperation. After the devastation of two world wars, a new dawn of governance appeared imminent—one that was shaped by ideals of democracy, human rights, and economic prosperity. Yet, despite the formation of multilateral institutions like the United Nations, World Trade Organization, and International Monetary Fund, many of the promises that these institutions and their Western sponsors put forth have remained unfulfilled.

The Promise of Democracy

One of the most persistent narratives championed by Western powers was that democracy would flourish as the dominant political system, promoting peace, development, and human rights. This promise was often accompanied by a discourse on the inevitability of liberal democratic systems triumphing over authoritarian and dictatorial regimes. The West, particularly after the Cold War, viewed itself as the beacon of this political ideal. The collapse of the Soviet Union was widely interpreted as the "end of history," with liberal democracy expected to sweep across the globe in its wake.

However, the implementation of democracy, especially in the Global South, was met with numerous challenges. Western interventions in countries like Iraq, Libya, and Afghanistan, ostensibly to promote democracy, often led to chaos, civil unrest, and in many cases, the emergence of regimes that were less democratic than the ones they replaced. For example, the U.S.-led invasion of Iraq in 2003 was sold to the international community as a necessary intervention to topple a tyrannical regime and instill democracy. However, the power vacuum that followed led to sectarian violence, the rise of extremist groups such as ISIS, and a protracted civil conflict that continues to destabilize the region today.

The broken promise of democracy is evident in how Western powers often prioritize strategic interests over genuine democratic reform. In countries where democracy might undermine their geopolitical goals, Western governments have supported authoritarian leaders and repressive regimes. Egypt, for instance, saw the West backing the military regime that overthrew the country's first democratically elected president in 2013, in part due to concerns over the rise of political Islam. Similarly, in countries like Saudi Arabia and Bahrain, democratic movements have been suppressed with Western acquiescence because of these nations' strategic importance.

Thus, while democracy is held up as a moral imperative by Western leaders, its promotion has often been inconsistent, selective, and in many cases, detrimental to the very populations it was supposed to benefit. This selective approach to democracy has led to disillusionment across the Global South, as people have come to view Western promises of political reform with skepticism and mistrust.

The Economic Promises of Globalization

In tandem with the promotion of democracy, Western nations have been ardent advocates of globalization. The promise was simple: global economic integration would lead to widespread prosperity, lifting millions out of poverty and fostering economic development across the world. Trade liberalization, open markets, and foreign investment were seen as pathways toward a more interconnected, equitable, and prosperous world.

However, the reality of globalization has been far more complex, with benefits disproportionately accruing to wealthier nations and multinational corporations. Developing countries, especially in Africa and Latin America, have often found themselves at the mercy of international trade systems that favor Western economies. The removal of trade barriers and the insistence on free-market reforms by institutions like the World Bank and IMF, as conditions for financial aid, have often left these nations more impoverished, with weakened local industries and rising inequality.

The structural adjustment programs (SAPs) imposed by Western-led financial institutions in the 1980s and 1990s are emblematic of the broken promises of economic liberalization. Countries that accepted these programs, such as Zambia and Ghana, were required to slash public spending, deregulate markets, and open up to foreign investment. While these measures were intended to stabilize economies and attract foreign investment, they often had the opposite effect. Public services deteriorated, industries were decimated by competition from cheap foreign goods, and unemployment soared. In many cases, the Western companies and investors benefited, while local economies suffered.

The global financial crisis of 2008 further exposed the flaws in the Western-driven economic order. The crisis, which originated in the financial hubs of the West, particularly in the United States, sent shockwaves across the globe, devastating economies far removed from the epicenter. Developing countries, which had been encouraged to integrate into the global financial system, were left to bear the brunt of the economic downturn, despite having played no role in its creation. This crisis underscored the vulnerability of the Global South to the whims of Western financial systems, shattering the illusion that globalization would lead to shared prosperity.

The Broken Promise of Climate Action

As the world grapples with the devastating impacts of climate change, another broken promise looms large: the commitment of Western nations to lead the fight against global warming. The industrialization of the West, which relied heavily on fossil fuels, is responsible for much of the greenhouse gas emissions that have led to the current climate crisis. Yet, despite their historical responsibility, Western countries have been slow to take meaningful action, often prioritizing short-term economic gains over long-term environmental sustainability.

The Paris Agreement of 2015 was hailed as a historic moment in the fight against climate change, with world leaders pledging to limit global temperature rise to below 2 degrees Celsius. However, in the years since, many Western countries have failed to meet their emissions reduction targets. The United States, under the Trump administration, even withdrew from the agreement entirely, signaling a retreat from global climate leadership. Although the U.S. has since rejoined the agreement under the Biden administration, the damage to global trust remains.

Meanwhile, developing countries, which have contributed far less to global emissions, are bearing the brunt of climate change's impacts, from rising sea levels in the Pacific islands to devastating droughts in Africa. Western nations have promised financial aid to help these countries adapt to the changing climate, but the funds have often been slow to materialize, or have come with strings attached. For example, the $100 billion per year promised by developed nations to support climate adaptation in developing countries has yet to be fully realized, leaving many vulnerable communities without the resources they need to protect themselves.

In the absence of strong leadership from the West, emerging powers like China have sought to position themselves as leaders in the fight against climate change. However, China's continued reliance on coal and its role in financing fossil fuel projects in developing countries through initiatives like the Belt and Road Initiative complicate its claims to climate leadership. The failure of both Western and emerging powers to take decisive action on climate change raises serious questions about the future of global environmental governance and the ability of the international community to address one of the most pressing challenges of our time.

The Erosion of Multilateralism

The promise of multilateralism—international cooperation through institutions like the United Nations, the World Trade Organization, and the World Health Organization—has been a cornerstone of the Western-led global order. These institutions were designed to foster cooperation, resolve conflicts, and promote shared global goals, from poverty reduction to disease eradication. However, in recent years, multilateralism has come under increasing strain, with Western countries often undermining the very institutions they helped create.

One of the most glaring examples of this erosion is the weakening of the World Trade Organization (WTO). Established to regulate global trade and resolve disputes, the WTO has been sidelined by the rise of bilateral and regional trade agreements, many of which are dominated by Western powers and exclude developing countries. The United States, under both the Obama and Trump administrations, has been particularly critical of the WTO, accusing it of being ineffective and biased against American interests. By blocking the appointment of judges to the WTO's dispute resolution body, the U.S. has effectively crippled the institution, leaving many trade disputes unresolved and raising the specter of a return to protectionist policies.

The United Nations, too, has struggled to maintain its relevance in an increasingly fragmented world. The Security Council, dominated by the five permanent members (the U.S., the U.K., France, China, and Russia), has often been paralyzed by geopolitical rivalries, rendering it unable to address major global crises, from the Syrian civil war to the Rohingya genocide in Myanmar. The lack of reform in the UN system, particularly the overrepresentation of Western powers in key decision-making bodies, has led to growing calls from the Global South for a more inclusive and equitable system of global governance.

The COVID-19 pandemic has further exposed the weaknesses of multilateralism. While the World Health Organization (WHO) played a critical role in coordinating the global response to the pandemic, it was hamstrung by political infighting and underfunding. The U.S. withdrawal from the WHO in 2020, though temporary, highlighted the fragility of global health governance and the dangers of nationalism in a time of global crisis. Moreover, the uneven distribution of vaccines, with wealthy Western countries hoarding doses while poorer nations struggled to access them, underscored the deep inequalities in the global health system and the failure of Western nations to uphold their commitments to global solidarity.

As the world enters a new era of geopolitical competition, economic inequality, and environmental crisis, the future of global governance remains uncertain. The rise of new powers such as China, India, and other emerging economies has challenged the Western-dominated system of global governance that has been in place since the end of World War II. These new powers are increasingly demanding a greater say in global decision-making, and their rise presents both opportunities and challenges for the future of global governance.

China, in particular, has positioned itself as a major player on the world stage, challenging the hegemony of the United States and other Western powers. Through initiatives such as the Belt and Road Initiative (BRI), China has extended its influence across Asia, Africa, and Europe, offering an alternative model of development that contrasts sharply with the Western neoliberal model. The BRI, while criticized for creating debt dependencies, has provided much-needed infrastructure and investment in developing countries that have been neglected by Western financial institutions. As China continues to expand its economic and political reach, it will inevitably play a more prominent role in shaping the future of global governance.

However, the rise of new powers has also led to increased geopolitical tensions. The United States and its allies have viewed China's growing influence with suspicion, leading to a new era of great power competition reminiscent of the Cold War. This rivalry threatens to undermine the multilateral institutions that are already struggling to maintain relevance in a changing world. The failure of Western powers to accommodate the rise of new powers and reform global institutions to reflect the realities of the 21st century has only exacerbated this tension.

Beyond geopolitics, the challenge of inequality continues to plague global governance. The disparities between rich and poor nations have only deepened in recent decades, despite the promises of globalization and economic liberalization. Western countries have often used international institutions to maintain their economic dominance, ensuring that the rules of the global economy are skewed in their favor. This has led to growing resentment in the

Global South, where many feel that they have been excluded from the benefits of the global system.

The COVID-19 pandemic further illustrated these inequalities. While wealthy countries were able to rapidly develop and distribute vaccines, poorer nations were left waiting, with many still struggling to vaccinate their populations. The failure to address these disparities has undermined the credibility of Western-led global institutions and raised questions about their ability to respond to future crises. The pandemic has also highlighted the need for reform in global health governance, as the World Health Organization and other institutions struggled to coordinate an effective response in the face of political interference and a lack of resources.

Looking forward, the future of global governance will likely depend on the ability of the international community to reform existing institutions and create new ones that are better suited to the challenges of the 21st century. This will require Western powers to relinquish some of their dominance and work with emerging powers to create a more inclusive and equitable system of global governance. It will also require addressing the root causes of inequality, from unfair trade practices to the disproportionate impact of climate change on developing countries.

In addition, the rise of new technologies such as artificial intelligence and the increasing interconnectedness of the global economy present new challenges for global governance. These technologies have the potential to revolutionize industries and improve living standards, but they also raise important ethical and regulatory questions that the current global governance system is ill-equipped to handle. For example, the rise of automation threatens to displace millions of workers, particularly in developing countries that rely on low-wage labor. Without a coordinated global response, the benefits of these technologies are likely to accrue disproportionately to wealthy countries and multinational corporations, exacerbating existing inequalities.

Climate change, too, will continue to shape the future of global governance. The failure of Western countries to take meaningful action on climate change has already eroded trust in the global system, and the worsening impacts of global warming will only increase pressure on international institutions to act. The need for a just transition to a low-carbon economy that does not leave behind developing countries will be one of the defining challenges of the 21st century. Without greater cooperation between rich and poor nations, the international community risks further fragmentation and the collapse of multilateralism altogether.

Ultimately, the future of global governance will depend on the willingness of countries to cooperate in the face of common challenges. The broken promises of the past, whether in the areas of democracy promotion, economic development, or climate action, have left many disillusioned with the current system. However, the rise of new powers and the growing interconnectedness of the world provide an opportunity to rethink and reshape global governance for the better. If the international community can rise to the occasion, it may be possible to build a more just, equitable, and sustainable global order. If not, the world risks descending into a new era of conflict, inequality, and environmental degradation.

As the 21st century progresses, it is clear that the old order is no longer fit for purpose. The broken promises of the West have left a vacuum in global leadership that new powers are eager to fill. Whether this transition will lead to a more inclusive system of global governance or a return to great power rivalry and fragmentation remains to be seen. What is certain is that the future of global governance will be shaped by the choices that are made today, and the stakes have never been higher.

Conclusion

The narrative of Western dominance over the last century has been one of grand promises and deep contradictions. From the ideological battles of the Cold War to the promises of globalization and democratization, the Western-led global order has wielded immense influence over the course of world events. Yet, as this book has detailed, the promises made by Western powers have often fallen short, leading to a complex tapestry of broken commitments and unforeseen consequences.

As we reflect on the overarching themes of this book, it becomes clear that the Western vision for global governance—one marked by democracy, economic liberalization, and environmental stewardship—has been marred by inconsistencies, selective application, and, at times, outright failure. The initial optimism surrounding the post-World War II global order, which sought to promote peace, development, and cooperation through institutions like the United Nations and the Bretton Woods system, has given way to a more somber reality.

The promise of democracy, once envisioned as a universal ideal that would bring about a more just and peaceful world, has often clashed with the strategic interests of Western powers. While the narrative of democracy's triumph seemed almost inevitable in the immediate aftermath of the Cold War, the reality has proved far more complex. Western interventions, ostensibly aimed at promoting democratic values, have frequently led to destabilization and conflict. The cases of Iraq, Libya, and Afghanistan illustrate how the imposition of Western-style democracy without regard for local contexts and conditions can result in chaos and suffering rather than the promised stability and prosperity. This dissonance between proclaimed ideals and actual outcomes has contributed to growing disillusionment in many parts of the world, where democracy is seen not as a universal right but as a tool of Western dominance.

In parallel, the economic promises of globalization—centered around the belief that free markets and open trade would lead to widespread prosperity—have also been challenged by real-world outcomes. The neoliberal agenda, championed by Western powers and international financial institutions, promised economic development and poverty alleviation through structural adjustments and market liberalization. However, these policies often exacerbated inequalities and undermined local economies in the Global South. The structural adjustment programs of the 1980s and 1990s, which imposed harsh austerity measures and economic reforms on developing countries, frequently led to social upheaval and economic instability rather than the promised growth. The 2008 financial crisis further exposed the vulnerabilities and inequities inherent in the global economic system, revealing how interconnected financial markets can amplify crises and disproportionately impact less wealthy nations.

The environmental promises made by Western leaders have similarly failed to meet expectations. The industrialization of the West, which has been a major driver of climate change, stands in stark contrast to the slow and insufficient actions taken to address the crisis. The Paris Agreement, while a significant diplomatic achievement, has not been matched by the necessary commitments and actions to limit global warming effectively. The failure to address climate change comprehensively and equitably has left many developing countries, which contribute minimally to global emissions but face the brunt of climate impacts, vulnerable and underserved. This disconnect between Western promises and the harsh realities faced by vulnerable populations highlights the need for a more just and inclusive approach to environmental governance.

The erosion of multilateralism, which was once seen as a cornerstone of the post-World War II order, further underscores the challenges facing global governance. The weakening of institutions such as the World Trade Organization and the United Nations reflects broader geopolitical shifts and the growing reluctance of Western powers to uphold the principles of international cooperation. The rise of unilateral actions and protectionist policies undermines the ability of global institutions to address transnational challenges effectively. The COVID-19 pandemic has accentuated these issues, demonstrating how global health governance can be compromised by political and economic interests, leaving many countries inadequately prepared to respond to crises.

Looking to the future, the question of how global governance will evolve remains open. The rise of new powers, such as China and India, offers both opportunities and challenges for reshaping the global order. These emerging powers are not only seeking a greater role in global decision-making but also presenting alternative models of development and governance. China's Belt and Road Initiative, for example, represents a different approach to international engagement, offering infrastructure and investment in regions often neglected by Western-led institutions. However, this rise also brings its own set of challenges and controversies, including concerns over debt dependency and geopolitical competition.

The persistent inequalities and injustices within the global system demand a rethinking of how governance is structured and how power is distributed. The promise of globalization, democratization, and environmental stewardship must be reexamined in light of their real-world impacts. To build a more equitable and sustainable global order, it is essential to address the root causes of these issues and work towards inclusive solutions that genuinely benefit all nations and populations.

The future of global governance will likely hinge on several critical factors. First, there must be a concerted effort to reform existing international institutions to better reflect the current geopolitical and economic realities. This includes making institutions like the United Nations and the World Trade Organization more representative and effective in addressing contemporary challenges. Second, there needs to be a commitment to addressing global inequalities, both economic and environmental. This involves not only providing support to developing countries but also ensuring that the benefits of technological advancements and economic growth are more evenly distributed.

Finally, a renewed focus on multilateralism and international cooperation will be crucial in navigating the complexities of the 21st century. The global community must move beyond unilateral actions and embrace collaborative approaches to tackling issues such as climate change, pandemics, and geopolitical conflicts. Building trust and fostering dialogue among nations will be essential for creating a more stable and just global order.

In conclusion, the story of Western hegemony and its impact on global governance is one of broken promises and profound challenges. The ideals of democracy, economic prosperity, and environmental stewardship have often clashed with the realities of power politics, economic interests, and geopolitical competition. As the world moves forward, it is imperative to learn from these experiences and strive for a global governance system that is more inclusive, equitable, and responsive to the needs of all people. The path to a better future lies in acknowledging past mistakes, embracing new perspectives, and working together to build a world that fulfills the promises once made and addresses the pressing challenges of our time.

END

Broken Promises: Western Hegemony and Global Turmoil

ABOUT THE AUTHOR

Jibril Mohamed Ahmed is a distinguished scholar and practitioner in International Relations, currently pursuing a PhD at Selinus University, Italy. His research critically examines the effects of foreign aid on political stability in Sub-Saharan Africa, focusing on Ethiopia, Nigeria, and South Sudan. He holds a Master's degree in Political Science and International Relations from Addis Ababa University and a Bachelor's in Public Administration from Rift Valley University. Jibril has served in various impactful roles, including Chief Executive Director at Abadir Development Association, Vice President at Ramaas University, and Consultant at J.D Consultancy Group. His experience also includes a tenure as Project Officer with the Somali Community in Ethiopia.

Jibril is the author of several notable works, including *"Somalia's Road to Democracy: A Journey of Hope and Perseverance"*, which explores the political evolution of Somalia, and *"Untold Truths"*, a critical examination of hidden narratives in regional politics. His writings contribute to a deeper understanding of global governance and development challenges.

His professional and personal experiences, shaped by his background as a refugee from Somalia, deeply inform his scholarly approach and commitment to addressing complex global issues.

Made in the USA
Columbia, SC
13 September 2024